THROUGH
THE
FIRE

FELICIA ALFORD

DEDICATION

I dedicate this book to my grandmother, Gloria Alford, in memory of her beloved children and husband, James E. Alford.

Writing this book has definitely been one of the most difficult, life-altering, and transitioning journeys of my life. At times, the overwhelming pain and heartache of it all led to extreme bouts of mental distress and isolation. It was during those surreal escapes from my reality that I began to meditate and start doing the inner work of digging deep, peeling back layer after layer, and allowing myself to go within and face my fears, thereby finding the strength and courage, and most of all, discovering the FAITH, to complete the process, no matter what unforeseen obstacles or setbacks I may encounter.

It registered loud and clear what was required of me to do next. I simply went into "The ROOM" (better known as "The CLOSET" to most folks) in absolute submission, humbly bowed on bended knee. I called upon GOD and my angels above to grant me their blessing, order my steps, and give me divine guidance, as I went forth, exuding respect and integrity, determined to successfully execute what I call "My Labor of Love."

Mission accomplished, Grandma,
I love you!

ACKNOWLEDGEMENTS

First and foremost, I would like to thank God for giving me the strength and will power to embark on this journey.

My children Ryan and Sidney-Keith, you are the very reason and a constant reminder of why I continue to put one foot in front of the other each and every day!

My mother, Joan Alford and my uncle, Derrick Alford, the love and support shown by you two along this journey has truly been a treasured experience.

Mr. Spencer Leak Sr., I especially thank you for being such an inspiration and a wealth of knowledge. I greatly appreciate your attributes to this project.

Mr. Spencer Leak Jr., You've often said; The Alford family is very much a part of the Leak family's history. I say, The Leak family is very much a part of the Alford family's past, present and future. For all that you've done and all that you continue to do... I thank you!

Mr. James O'Grady, I thank you for embracing me and for the depth of insight you've given to me. Words cannot describe my gratitude.

Deborah L. Harris, CEO of Brand N Stone Publishing, your partnership with this project has been nothing short of a blessing given to me.

Atty, Keith L. Spence, I thank you for your continuous support and legal counsel.

The Alford Family:
Know that this story is "your" story.

Derrick Alford, (Son) Devin Alford

Denise Alford

My daughter Ryan Alford & son, Sidney-Keith Alford

Darryl Alford,(Wife) Sheemya Alford, Daughter- Aazja Alford,
Son – Amari Alford

Keith Alford, Sons- Kierce Alford and Kade Alford

To My Extended Family:
Thank you for your never ending love and support.

Bertha Alford, Oceaneak Alford, Jermika Alford, Karen Alford

Joyce Brice, Rose Andrews, Doris Andrews and James Andrews,

To anyone I have missed know that you are appreciated!

TABLE OF CONTENTS

PREFACE

The decision to write this book and tell my family's story took months of contemplating, as I was uncertain whether to dig so deeply in my soul and reveal such devastation, considering I'm a private person. The question I floundered with was, did I really want to allow people to gain insight into me and know about my family and our history? There are people in my life who would arguably contest to knowing everything about me. But they will be shocked to learn of this story. Allowing myself to be vulnerable has always been quite difficult for me. I pondered how other family members may react to reliving the catastrophe. Nevertheless, I decided to tell this story, which will remain a secret from most people in my life until the book's actual release.

The determining factor in writing this book was an overwhelming feeling that can only be described as being guided by the Divine to do so. I learned it was my grandmother's wishes that her children never be forgotten, as they were such beautiful souls that represented love and joy to her. I didn't realize that years ago she gave me everything I needed to tell this story. She never revealed the reason for providing me with this pertinent information and I never questioned it. Instead, I want future generations to comprehend the importance of our family's history. It's imperative that they know that survival and perseverance are qualities that travel throughout their veins. The idea of my children and generations to come learning of their heritage through a book written by me gives me immense gratification.

The tragedy surrounding my grandparents' legacy taught us that we can overcome difficult challenges by having faith the size of a mustard seed and by keeping God first. My grandfather often told me that life goes on and we must move on with it, that even in the midst of the storm, to never let go of God's unchanging hand, because in your darkest hours, he'll see you through. I often reflect and draw upon those words of wisdom to get me through adversity and disappointments in my times of trials and tribulations. This book represents the Alfords' journey of faith, hope, fear, and most of all, survival!

—*Felicia Alford*

INTRODUCTION

A frigid 10 degrees on February 21st, 1964, to most Chicagoans, was nothing more than a typical brutal winter night. But in a particular West Side neighborhood, that night will always be remembered as the time when a cataclysmic event occurred that changed a family's life forever. Eerie darkness and ferocious weather conditions had this buzzing city devoid of any movement. The faint wind that traveled through the air was the only sound to permeate the silence of the 41st block of Gladys Avenue. On the same street tucked away inside a bungalow resided a highly decorated Chicago detective and his family. Everyone inside of this loving home was in a peaceful sea of dreams, when suddenly, a woman screamed, "Fire!" Her bone-chilling voice echoed through the room, snapping the detective right out of a sound sleep.

He quickly bolted to his feet with his eyes fixed on the ember glow illuminating from a room across from theirs. At first, it seemed like a figment of his imagination until he opened the door and flames shot right in his face. In less than minutes, the fire took on a life of its own, moving at an incredible speed. Time was of the essence, as the detective raced through the house, shouting instructions, hollering names, knowing that he was working against the clock. Although his profession afforded him knowledge and tools to handle crisis situations, he never envisioned that a disaster such as this would come crashing under his own roof.

The fire began to burn with such intensity that in a blink of an eye it turned into a dangerous escape from death. Clouds of smoke quickly erupted in the air, making his vision become extremely blurry. He desperately fought his way through the flames that sizzled and popped like fireworks. The temperature was excruciatingly hot, and it became quite difficult to breathe, but the mission to get everyone to safety couldn't be compromised. The pressure was escalating and the seconds were ticking. Then there was a loud boom, which neighbors later described as equivalent to the sound of an explosive stick of dynamite.

Onlookers helplessly stood watching, oblivious to the freezing cold, as the flames engulfed all sides of the house. It seemed forever and a day before loud fire truck sirens came blaring through the streets. Soon the lingering smell of smoke took over the neighborhood. Black dust floated in the air and the charred remains of the house stood like a skeleton. The vision was too much to take in, as they shook their heads in disbelief, watching a family's priceless memories, dreams, hopes, and aspirations destroyed, leaving only painful regrets and sorrow, never to be forgotten.

THE ALFORDS

Birmingham, Alabama, in 1926, marked a time in history in which African Americans lived in the Jim Crow era, when laws were enforced to uphold racial segregation in the South. The extremes to keep blacks and whites divided included separate schools, marked signs, and curfews, just to a name a few. Although slavery was abolished, the inferior treatment of blacks remained.

The reinforcement of segregation was apparent in the 1926 case of Wyatt versus Adair, a court battle between two white men in the city of Birmingham. A summary of the case is as follows: W.P. Wyatt leased a store and residential floor to J.E. Adair. He later leased another floor in the same house to a black family. Adair viewed this as an outrageous act of cruelty and a blatant disrespect to whites. His anger stemmed from having only one bathroom in the residence. Adair moved out and sued Wyatt, citing his family suffered mental anguish being in such close proximity to blacks. The U.S. Supreme Court supported his claim and ruled that individuals could agree privately not to rent or sell to blacks. Adair was awarded monetary damages for moving expenses, lost rent, and humiliation. It was noted from that case that the courts would intervene if individuals violated the norms of segregation. In the same year, coded zoning maps developed. Their purpose was to provide an area in Birmingham where blacks were permitted to live under a local law. These are just a couple of examples of the hardships African Americans endured at that time in Birmingham, Alabama, a city looked upon back then as the most segregated place in America.

It was during those unfavorable conditions that James Edward Alford Jr. was born. He was known as Jimmy as soon as he came out of the womb. He was the second son of James Alford Sr. and Martha Lovejoy Alford. While Jimmy and his brother, Billy, were still small children, their father, James Sr., was involved in a racial altercation with a few white men that could have produced deadly consequences. Therefore, it caused James to go on the run for his life and forced him to leave his family behind. He assumed another identity and unfortunately was never heard from again. Martha stayed in Birmingham, raising her two sons, until she made a decision to relocate.

Jimmy was just entering grade school when his family moved to Pittsburgh, Pennsylvania, in search of greater opportunities. They didn't escape racial discrimination, and blacks were still fighting to knock down the walls of segregation. But the black community was growing rapidly, attributable to higher paying wages in this industrial city. This was a place known for its steelmaking, and along with that, the coal miners provided more economic growth. Clouds of smoke hung over the city during work hours, but it was still worth fleeing from the callous treatment in the South. The Alford name set a principle of striving for excellence early in Jimmy's childhood. He received his high school diploma, and after graduating, enlisted in the U.S. Navy. Jimmy developed a real sense of purpose in the military. Three years of service contributed to his strong sense of commitment, honor, and courage.

After he left the Navy, Jimmy relocated to Chicago, a city that became the cornerstone for creating the Alford legacy. It was in the late forties when Jimmy joined his family there. By this time, an astronomical number of blacks had migrated to Chicago from the South. Although struggle and intolerance still pervaded the black community, blacks were determined to create an avenue for themselves in this big city of opportunity. African Americans quickly became a substantial urban population on Chicago's South and West Sides. There were designated neighborhoods on the South Side of town labeled "The Black Belt" of Chicago. This segregation of class, according to economic status, brought on an urgent response to invigorate black businesses and entrepreneurs. In addition, it generated a feeling of unity and established communities that were groundbreaking for the advancement of the black race.

The Alford family skill set afforded them the luxury of living above the poverty line. Jimmy's mother, Lovejoy, began her career as a seamstress, and his employment history embarked with the Chicago Transit Authority as a bus driver. Jimmy adjusted to his new home with a mindset and appetite aimed toward success. In time, a beautiful young lady caught his eye named Gloria Esther Johnson, known to her family and close friends as Glo. They began dating and soon became inseparable. Glo, being a native of Chicago, took pleasure in familiarizing Jimmy with the city.

The social life for African Americans centered on music. It was an escape from the harsh realities they faced on a continuous basis. It didn't matter if it was the dirty blues in the bars and lounges, the mellow jazz in the nightclubs, where people dressed in their fancy clothing, or the gospel music at Sunday morning services, where most of the leading artists were introduced to the music world. It was the church where some of the most renowned musicians in history got their start. African Americans were also becoming prolific in the literary world depicting life in the urban ghetto. Most known for her outstanding work is Chicago native, Gwendolyn Brooks, who in 1950 became the first African American woman to be honored with the Pulitzer Prize.

Blacks were progressing in a society designed toward betterment. Jimmy and Glo's courtship eventually led to marriage, and their first child, Keith Alford, was born June 7th, 1950. Jimmy quickly embraced his role as a family man and sought higher paying wages. His persistence paid off just in time for them to welcome their second child, Jimmy Alford Jr., who was born in 1952. He then became employed as a Chicago police officer. The U.S. Navy had given him the foundation needed to smoothly transition to his role as a police officer. He understood the responsibilities attached to upholding an oath to serve and protect.

Jimmy launched his career as an officer in the 24th District in Lawndale. However, there was racial tension within the organization, as black officers were unable to arrest white citizens and black leaders couldn't exercise their authority over white officers. Although African Americans were better represented in the police force in Chicago than in any other big city, they were unfortunately slowly promoted. However, Jimmy didn't allow any stumbling blocks to distract him from his ultimate goal. He had a duty to his family and now to the city of Chicago!

In 1955, the Alfords' third child and first daughter, Denise Alford, was born. Jimmy's diligence to the workforce allowed Glo to be a stay-at-home mom and homemaker. Her dedication to her family never wavered. She made sure Jimmy and the kids were well taken care of. The Alfords were quite familiar with the two sides of town where blacks were welcomed, which were south and west, the early part of their marriage being spent on Chicago's West Side. Small residential units comprised both areas. That kept the Alfords in search of more space to accommodate their growing family.

That time also marked the birth of the civil rights movement, which centered on three major areas of discrimination: education, segregation in public places, and the right to vote. The crusade for equality made blacks more powerful than ever. The idea of a movement being executed without violence only magnified their threat. Great leaders such as Dr. Martin Luther King Jr., John Lewis, and Roy Wilkins revised the destiny of the black race in America. Their voices were instrumental in changing laws and making history. They were also able to establish the value of the black dollar.

The Montgomery bus boycott lasted more than a year, forcing the U.S. Supreme Court to rule that segregated seating was unconstitutional. The boycott was sparked by an African American woman named Rosa Parks refusing to give up her seat to a white man after a long day of work and move to the back of the bus. She was arrested and the outrage in the African American community resulted in blacks finding alternative travel plans until their demands were granted. Rosa Parks' bold stand in violating the segregation law made her a nationally recognized symbol of dignity and strength and a hero in the black community.

The Alfords continued with their normal routine, and Glo gave birth to three children over the next consecutive years. Kelvin Alford was born in 1956, Patricia Alford in 1957, and Steven Alford in 1958. During that time, the Alford family lived in an apartment building on the West Side, where they developed an everlasting bond with the Andrews family that lived beneath them. Both families were rather large and the Alfords' oldest son, Keith, and the Andrews' oldest son, Otis, became great friends, which had a domino effect on the other children gravitating to one another.

The unique common denominator was that both families were raised in a two-parent household. It only made the connection closer and more grounded. The children spent quality time under the upbringing of the Alfords and the Andrews. However, a great amount of their time was spent under the supervision of Mrs. Andrews, known as "MaDear" (Mother-Dear). She was such a warm, open-hearted woman that all of the kids in the neighborhood loved her.

Although Glo was a stay-at-home mom, it was MaDear's house where the kids spent most of their time playing. It could have been that she had more insight into what was transpiring in the outside world. Glo, on the other hand, was more cautious and lived her life through her husband, Jimmy. Her entire world centered on her family and she had no desire to work outside of the home. She was simply a loving person who knew how to treat people. Her doors were always open to anyone who needed a helping hand. Glo was the type of woman you could talk to about anything. She always tried to give the best advice to anyone seeking her opinion. Glo didn't care if a person had to seek assistance from her over and over again. She allotted as much time as was needed to keep a person on the right track. Both mothers were great cooks, but Glo ranked among the best in the city of Chicago. One of her specialties was the recipe she developed for yeast rolls. They were so delicious that the rolls melted right in your mouth. This structured foundation from both families allowed the children to be raised in a stable and loving environment.

The Andrews had a daughter named JoAnn, who would later in life reacquaint with the Alfords in such a divine way. Denise, the Alfords' oldest daughter, was such a beautiful and shy little girl growing up. She would just tickle MaDear each time she asked for bread and jelly because she pronounced it "bread and delly." MaDear would have to listen closely and get her to repeat certain things to be able to understand her words. Denise was adorable and did her best in assisting Glo with her younger siblings. She was even part of the groundbreaking ceremony for Melody Elementary School. A couple of six-year-old students were selected and lifted first shovels of dirt on a construction site located at 412 S. Keeler Avenue. Denise's picture was featured in the newspaper for her participation on that memorable occasion. Then there was Jimmy, who was a very handsome and outgoing young boy. He was always into something and captured everyone's attention with his confident presence. He was jokingly labeled "Tommy Tucker the bad mother****!" He was very meticulous with his clothing and had a knack for winning people over, even at such a young age.

MaDear and Glo loved their children immensely, which often meant undying and unspoken sacrifices. They met their children's needs before they catered to their own. It meant their kids ate before an ounce of food touched their mouths. They, along with the bread winners of the household, maintained a place to definitely call home. The tight connection between the families continued until the Andrews family moved away.

By this time, Jimmy's level of achievement as an officer earned him a promotion to detective. He quickly became acquainted with the new sergeant of the robbery division, Sergeant James O'Grady, a man destined to move up the ranks in the department. They immediately formed a respectful supervisory-subordinate relationship. O'Grady admitted that in the beginning Jimmy actually knew more about robbery than he did. He regarded Jimmy as an officer that was always a step ahead and didn't require supervision. Jimmy by far exceeded his responsibilities of conducting follow-up investigations related to criminal offenses. He had an advantage in the streets being such a people person. Jimmy embraced individuals from all walks of life, and along with that, had an outgoing personality and a bright smile. He also had credible informants who kept him updated on the movement in the streets. It was a perfect time for Jimmy to receive a promotion as his family increased.

The Alfords took a two-year break before their next two children were born. Tyrone Alford was born in 1960 and Christina Alford was born in 1962. In that same year, Jimmy picked up a second job with the U.S. Postal Service on Van Buren and Canal. He worked the morning shift because of his afternoon hours with the police department. The Alfords had dreams of purchasing their own property and began saving toward that end. They eventually found a two-story brick building on the West Side, located on 41st and Gladys, with an option to own. The building contained five rooms downstairs, which included the living room, dining room, bathroom, the Alfords' bedroom, and a guestroom. The upstairs had two rooms with huge open space, which was going to be the children's quarters. The only thing missing was an upstairs bathroom, which was a renovation Jimmy planned to make once they purchased the property.

Their new living space was large enough to keep the family from feeling cramped like the prior places. The children being so close in age had a tight bond as they grew up together. Keith took his responsibility as being the big brother quite seriously and had no problem helping his younger siblings. The Alford name became well known in the educational system once the children became of school age, each one following a set of footprints, but at the same time, creating their own identity. The Alfords continued to provide their kids with the nourishment and love needed to maintain a good upbringing.

Jimmy learned a lot about his surroundings from the time he spent at the neighborhood tavern. Van Keeler's Lounge was located in a big building down the street from the Alfords' home. On one side of the lounge was the bar and on the other side was the neighborhood grocery store. The second level of the building was used to rent out for functions such as banquets, wedding receptions, and other special occasions. Inside the front entrance of the tavern, there was a front counter, where you could purchase alcohol to go, and an old jukebox was set in the corner to play music at the establishment.

The owner of the tavern, Bucky, was Jimmy's additional eyes and ears there. Jimmy was also closely connected with a couple of guys who were regular patrons at the bar named L.A. and Westbrook. They enjoyed shooting the breeze with Jimmy over a cold beer, while keeping him updated on the news around the neighborhood. People automatically gravitated to Jimmy because he was simply a man who knew everything from his point of view. He could speak on a variety of topics that ranged from politics and law to religion. It didn't matter what the subject was, as Jimmy always had an opinion and had no problem expressing it. His ability to capture an audience made him quite a popular man, and the patrons loved to see him walk through the tavern door. Jimmy's presence also brought a sense of calmness and protection to the tavern, since an officer of the law was on hand. The Alfords continued to settle in their new house with love and laughter as time traveled on.

In the summer of 1963, the most iconic and defining speech was delivered from the steps of the Lincoln Memorial in Washington, D.C. Civil Rights Activist, Dr. Martin Luther King Jr., addressed a crowd of more than 250,000 people to demand jobs and freedom. It was here that he delivered the "I Have a Dream" speech. Dr. King filled African Americans across the country with hope and a promise for a brighter tomorrow. The part of Dr. King's speech that most excited the crowd was when he described his dreams of freedom and equality arising in a land that included slavery, as well as hatred. Dr. King joined the likes of Jefferson and Lincoln in the ranks of men responsible for shaping America. His famous powerful words of being able to join hands brought on a deeper unity within the black race.

Later that fall in Chicago there was a public school boycott known as "Freedom Day." It was a demonstration that kept more than 200,000 students from school. The problem was that classrooms were overcrowded and there were not enough textbooks for students. In hopes to end segregation in the city schools, more than 10,000 protestors marched downtown to the Chicago Board of Education offices. Blacks were making a statement across the country for equality and were determined not to be ignored. Jimmy and Glo were among the majority that was enthused over the changes that were occurring for black people in America.

It was early November of 1963, the time of year when gold- and rust-colored autumn leaves scattered the dry pavements. The Thanksgiving holiday was right around the corner, a holiday in which gratitude was expressed for family, friends, and health. Furthermore, it was a time to extend a helping hand to the less fortunate, an endeavor the Alfords practiced relentlessly. Their home remained open for people to share in the love, laughter, and hot meals that occurred behind their front door. It was also a time for Glo to make her scrumptious sweet potato pie. Being the mother of eight children made her a nurturer by nature. She took pleasure in being a caregiver from the heart, and treating people with kindness was one of her most pronounced traits. Glo didn't complain one bit about being a homemaker and the fact that she totally depended on Jimmy. She never felt it necessary to even learn how to drive because her husband, along with other individuals, took her wherever she needed to go.

With their generous hearts, the Alfords were always looking to help out their fellow man during tough times. So, when Jimmy's cousins, Louise and her brother, Louis, showed up at the Alfords needing assistance, their altruism immediately kicked in. Louise and Louis were born in Birmingham, Alabama, like Jimmy, and relocated to Chicago for better opportunities.

They lived in the same building on the South Side right off 60th Street. Louise and Louis were both married with families now. Growing up, throughout the years, Jimmy's rapport was mostly with Louise and so he wasn't as familiar with Louis.

The one thing that Jimmy knew about Louis was his struggle with alcoholism. Louis had struggled with the addiction throughout the years, and it eventually led to a separation from his wife. His parents tried to help him by relocating him back to Birmingham, and they staged an intervention. They hoped if they supported Louis in this way it would help him straighten out his life, but Louis insisted he was okay and headed back to Chicago. Louis had been back for a few months before they showed up at the Alfords' doorstep. He had been living with Louise and her husband, but that living arrangement deteriorated once Louis's employment was terminated. A few prior incidents of violating the company's work policy eventually led to a heated exchange between Louis and his boss. As a result, he was let go at the restaurant.

The responsibility of feeding another mouth finally took a toll on Louise's husband. It caused constant bickering between the two and placed a tremendous strain on their marriage. Louise loved her brother, but her commitment was to the marriage vows she promised to honor to her husband. She didn't want to just toss Louis out on the street and prayed the Alfords would be able to provide him with temporary shelter. Louise and Louis assured Jimmy that his alcohol problem was under control. They were confident that once Louis obtained employment he would be back on his feet again. The Alfords had a private discussion, as they always did when making a major decision, and then agreed to assist Louis during this time of need.

Louis moved into the guestroom right across from the Alfords' bedroom. The room was already furnished, so he moved right in, with his personal belongings. Jimmy knew the battle that black men faced in America during that time. It was very grim and challenging for men who lacked adequate training and education in an unjust society. The first couple of weeks of Louis's stay, Jimmy passed on to him every lead that he came across for employment opportunities. But the harsh reality remained that Louis was a forty-year-old black man with an erratic work history and a substance-abuse issue. The Alfords made certain that Louis was given the privacy needed to climb out of the rut he appeared to be in. The children were not allowed to disturb him or visit his room. The only time Louis interacted with the children was basically at the dinner table.

It was shortly after that that Louis finally gained sporadic employment as a day laborer. He left at the crack of dawn to see if anyone on Workmen's Compensation needed his services for odd jobs. The Alfords knew Louis's income wasn't sufficient for him to contribute financially. Therefore, they allowed him to keep his money to save toward getting his own place. As time went by, Louis struggled to get over the hump.

Around the first of December, Louis began to patronize the local tavern on a regular basis. Jimmy had discussed with Bucky Louis's past alcohol struggles, asking him to keep an extra eye on him. He believed that Louis was reverting back to familiar territory and wanted Bucky to confirm his suspicion. The Alfords also began to discover empty wine bottles in their garbage from Louis obviously sneaking alcohol into his bedroom. He never allowed the Alfords to see his alcohol consumption, but they soon began to witness the effects. The Alfords were not condemning drinking, but escaping responsibility was unacceptable in their eyes. By Christmas time, Louis's drinking had escalated to the point that he became intoxicated on a regular basis. The reassurance that Louise and Louis had given Jimmy about his reformed ways seemed to be water under the bridge. His behavior eventually alarmed the Alfords and they put Louis on notice that his living arrangement was in jeopardy. The little money that Louis was hustling up was going mainly to support his drinking habit. The Alfords' patience was running thin and they refused to be a crutch in supporting Louis's destructive drinking habit.

Despite having to contend with their houseguest's heavy drinking, the Alfords recognized that there was something remarkable taking place for African Americans in 1964. The Civil Rights Act to end discrimination was before Congress, marking a landmark period for African Americans. The ordinance would end segregation in public places and employment discrimination on the basis of race, color, religion, sex, or natural origin. In spite of President John F. Kennedy's assassination on November 22nd, 1963, we can credit him for the initiation of the act. President Kennedy was publicly endorsed by Martin Luther King Sr., the father of the civil rights leader. In the 1960 election, more than 70 percent of African Americans

voted for Kennedy, and that support was instrumental in him beco
thirty-fifth president of the United States. However, it was his suc
President Lyndon Johnson, who would go on to sign the Civil Rights
into law. Blacks were inching closer to winning their fight to have equa
rights under the Constitution.

It was the first of the year and definitely a time for new beginnings. Life
was looking quite promising for the Alfords and their future appeared to be
heading in a favorable direction. They had a contract in place to purchase
the building and the reality of owning their own property seemed inevitable. The children were growing and their oldest son, Keith, was months
away from the adolescent stage. The only troublesome factor in their lives
stemmed from Louis's presence and his drinking. Their extended kindness
to help him get back on his feet had turned into a gesture of regret. He
remained unemployed and his heavy drinking continued. Most of his time
was spent at Van Keeler's Lounge, as it was within walking distance of the
Alfords. He was definitely a regular patron there, along with the woman
he befriended from the neighborhood. She was the mother of six, which
was something people found hard to believe with the hours she spent at
the tavern. Unfortunately, she and Louis seemed to be heading down the
same road of destruction.

The upcoming month would mark ninety days of Louis being the
Alfords' houseguest, which was adequate time to be on a path toward
betterment. However, this was something that Louis was failing to achieve.
Therefore, the time he spent at the Alfords was dwindling down to either
shape up or find another place to live. If he didn't comply, they were prepared
to orchestrate a plan for his departure without an ounce of guilt.

A FIERY TRAGEDY

The morning of February 20th, 1964, began as a typical morning in the Alford household. The strong aroma of breakfast cooking and coffee percolating traveled through the air. Preparing a hot and filling breakfast for the kids and Jimmy was a notable task that Glo engaged in with supreme dedication. The children of school age prepared for their day at Hefferan Elementary School, located on the 4400 block of West Wilcox Street. Everyone attended the school, with the exception of Keith, who was now in junior high. Nine-year-old Denise had contracted the mumps and had already missed a week of school. Glo noticed symptoms prior to the actual diagnosis from the doctor. Denise had swollen glands, a loss of appetite, and a slight fever. Being the mother of eight children kept her eyes keen and alert for anything out of the ordinary. It also allowed Glo to implement home remedies when the children became ill.

Jimmy's vacation from the police department was coming to an end. He had been away from the department since February 6th, but he was still obligated to his part-time job at the Post Office. He worked there from 9:00 a.m. to 1:00 p.m. Glo made sure the children were dressed warmly and she even reminded Jimmy to dress according to the weather. Once everyone was out the door, Glo diverted her attention to the smaller children and Denise's illness. Glo knew the illness would eventually run its course, and until then her job was to keep her as comfortable as possible. Louis remained in his room and probably had no plans on coming out until it was time for him to go to the tavern. There was no indication from Louis that he planned on changing his behavior. It appeared that drinking and chain-smoking cigarettes were his preferred lifestyle. The Alfords had discussed over the last couple of days that Louis's time at their home had reached the end of their rope.

A lot of excitement was stirring around at the Post Office because it was payday Friday. Jimmy ended his shift and executed his normal routine on payday, which was cash his check and go grocery shopping. He tried his best to assist Glo whenever possible because he knew the tremendous amount of responsibility she faced on a daily basis. Jimmy arrived home with the groceries before the children got out of school. He put the food away and got a quick update on Denise's condition.

Jimmy saw that Louis wasn't home and realized that his whereabouts wasn't a mystery. So, around 3:30 p.m., Jimmy decided to walk down to the neighborhood tavern. He walked into a mini crowd at Van Keeler's Lounge, which was common on Friday afternoons. Jimmy looked around until he spotted Bucky. He walked over to him and discussed some information with him concerning a case he was working on. Jimmy then observed Louis seated at the bar chugging down a beer. He talked to Bucky for about twenty minutes, and in that short timeframe, observed Louis on his third beer. Jimmy causally walked over to Louis and whispered in his ear for him to slow down because he was reaching his limit. He didn't even wait for Louis to respond because there was no justifiable excuse for Louis always drinking to intoxication. Jimmy joined Westbrook and L.A. for a beer at the bar. They sat around socializing and listening to the music from the jukebox like the other patrons scattered around.

Meanwhile, the children arrived home from school, and Glo realized that Jimmy had left bread from his grocery list. She left Keith in charge of the kids and made her way to the store next to the bar. Glo made her purchase and stepped into the bar to inform Jimmy that it would soon be dinnertime. Jimmy was engaged in a deep conversation with Bucky, L.A., and Westbrook, but he still acknowledged her presence. Glo looked around the establishment and observed Louis at the other end of the bar with a woman she was familiar with from the neighborhood. The woman had come by the Alfords' place on a few occasions to borrow some loose change from her. She didn't know much about her, except that a lot of her time was spent hanging out on the block. Glo walked to where she and Louis were seated. They insisted on purchasing Glo a beer, but she declined. She made her interaction with them very brief because she knew Louis was intoxicated. Glo went back and sat down next to Jimmy while she enjoyed a Coke. The Alfords hung around for another thirty minutes before they made their way home.

It was close to 4:30 p.m. when they walked through the door. Glo went upstairs to check on the children and found them working on their homework assignments while the younger kids played. Once Glo saw that everything was running normally, she went to the kitchen and made dinner. Jimmy went to relax in the living room, where he quickly dropped down in his easy chair and propped up his feet. It was a rare occasion that Jimmy got an opportunity to relax and he was taking full advantage of it. At around 5:30 p.m., the doorbell rang, and it was Westbrook and L.A. looking to pick back up their conversation with Jimmy. They brought over a six-pack of beer and sat around the front room talking. After a little while, Glo called the children to the dinner table. By now, Louis had made it home and came out of his room to join them.

It was obvious that he was quite intoxicated from his disheveled clothing, slurred speech, and the fact that he was having difficulty keeping a steady gait. Glo was disgusted by his presence and wanted him to hurry eating so he could get out of everyone's sight. Jimmy wasn't quite ready to eat and asked Glo if she could heat up his plate later. Westbrook and L.A. hung around for another hour or so before they made their departure. Jimmy finally came to the table to eat his dinner. He and Glo had a brief discussion concerning Louis's behavior. Glo was adamant about having a talk with Louis before the night ended. She had reached her limit with his behavior and wanted him out of their home. Jimmy agreed and retired to the bedroom to watch television.

At around 8:30 p.m., Glo got the children ready for bed. The renovations to the upstairs bathroom were still under construction, so the children were downstairs, taking turns bathing. The children hugged Jimmy good night, and Glo went upstairs to make sure everyone was tucked in for the night. On the right, there was a door to a large room. The room belonged to the girls and contained a baby bed for Christina and a full-size bed that Denise and Patricia shared. The room on the left belonged to the boys. Inside were two junior beds that belonged to twelve-year-old James Jr. and eight-year-old Kelvin. The other twin beds were occupied by five-year-old Stevie and three-year-old Tyrone. Keith slept alone in a twin-size bed near the door. The room also contained two dressers, a desk, and toys.

Glo checked Denise's temperature before kissing all the other kids good night. Then she went downstairs and walked into the kitchen to find Louis digging his hand in the pot on the stove. It perturbed her to no limit to see any unsanitary acts going on in her kitchen. Glo felt now was a good time to have a discussion with Louis. She simply told him it was time for him to stand on his own two feet and leave their home. Jimmy overheard the conversation and walked into the kitchen to support her decision. Louis agreed to leave and the Alfords retired to their bedroom. They climbed into bed and began watching television, as they heard Louis go in and out of the house a few times. They thought perhaps Louis was moving his belongings out, so they continued watching television until they fell asleep.

A tranquil stillness pervaded the house that night. The only sound traveling through the house was the howling wind beating against the windows. At around 1:15 a.m., the smell of fire permeated the room and awakened Glo. Realizing that it was in fact a fire, Glo screamed for Jimmy to wake up. He was slightly disoriented as he bolted to his feet, wearing only a T-shirt and shorts. Jimmy tried to clear his vision, since for a minute everything seemed blurry, until he focused on the ember glow coming from the guestroom. He sprinted across the room, grabbed his trousers, and slipped them on, as he dashed out of their room. Glo ran right behind him, and they observed Louis in the dining room, weaving around sloppy-drunk.

Glo screamed in Louis's face, "You started a fire!"

With no more time to waste, Jimmy swung Louis's bedroom door open, where he saw covers smoldering on the floor. With the aroma of fire beginning to fill the air, Jimmy noticed the mattress was missing from the bed. Louis told him it was in the bathtub, not realizing the severity of what was behind the door. Jimmy swung the bathroom door open. He was met by blazing flames burning him from the waist on up. Jimmy shouted for Glo to call the fire department, as flames shot across the wall, causing the drapes and furniture to catch fire.

Glo frantically grabbed the phone from the wall, but the line was dead. She ran out of the house, screaming for help, as she banged on a neighbor's door. Meanwhile, the flames had traveled to the staircase leading upstairs to where the children slept. The smoke was thick and heavy, as Jimmy fought his way **through the fire** to rescue the children. Louis followed behind Jimmy, still oblivious to the reason, considering the inebriated state he was in. The searing heat made it difficult for Jimmy to breathe, as he forced his way **through the fire**. Jimmy touched Stevie and Tyrone, but they were limp. He shouted their names through the agony of his weary voice, but no response. Jimmy moved to Keith's bed and slapped him until he woke up. He then snatched Jimmy Jr. out of bed and led him and Keith to the middle of the floor. Jimmy dashed to the window and fumbled through the darkness trying to open it. The window had a twist latch, as well as a weather strip, keeping Jimmy from being able to open it. With no time to waste, he took his bare foot and kicked the glass out of the pane. Jimmy pushed Keith and Jimmy Jr. toward the window to show them their escape. He prayed that they could rescue the other boys and make it onto the roof beyond the window to jump.

Desperate and determined, Jimmy fought his way through the dangerous fire to rescue his girls. He staggered to Denise's bed and tried to pick her up in his arms, but she was limp. Overcome by smoke, Jimmy fell to his knees and dropped his head on the bed. However, his will was stronger than his fear, as he pulled himself back up and made it to the window to create an escape. He pounded on it with the remaining strength he had left in his weakening body. He wasn't giving up trying to rescue his children, even if it meant at the cost of his own life. Jimmy finally knocked the center brace from the glass.

Before he could turn and make his way back to his daughters, a roaring sound came echoing in his ears. The air from the outside combined with the enclosed flames caused a combustion of heat, sending him sailing through the window with flames coming from his clothing. As Jimmy's body landed on the sidewalk, Glo rushed to his side. She quickly smothered the flames and pulled him to a tree, as painful screams traveled from her mouth and unstoppable tears flowed down her face. Jimmy hollered in agony, as he tried desperately to crawl back into the building. The Alfords helplessly watched their place engulfed in flames in complete shock, as they screamed and begged for someone to please help their children!

Finally, the loud sirens from the fire truck came blaring down the street. It was then that the Alfords spotted Keith standing in the passageway between the two buildings. He stood alone in a complete state of shock as he looked up at the burning building.

Glo yelled Keith's name, and he bewilderedly walked over to them.

Keith was traumatized and sadly asked his father, "Did you get any of them out?"

Jimmy, barely conscious, shook his head no, and before his head hit the ground, asked, "Where is Jimmy Jr.?"

Keith dropped his head in despair and shrugged his shoulders. It was later revealed that Keith had the two youngest boys, but Louis snatched them out of his arms, for a reason never to be justified. The family dog, Gaylord, appeared with his fur aflame, and was put to death by a compassionate policeman who put him out of his agony. The paramedics immediately placed Jimmy on a stretcher and put an oxygen mask over his face. He had inhaled a lot of smoke and was in and out of consciousness, as he was loaded in the back of the ambulance, along with Glo and Keith. An intravenous line was immediately placed in Jimmy's left arm to supply him with the fluids he lost. The ambulance sped away, as the brick foundation stood blackened around the empty openings that were once doors and windows. The lives lost were a haunting catastrophe that left an everlasting impact from a family's devastating misfortune.

3

PAINFUL GOODBYES

Once at the hospital, Jimmy was rushed straight into the trauma unit with severe second- degree burns and a broken leg. The doctors surrounded Jimmy's bedside as he went in and out of consciousness. They thought Jimmy had succumbed to his injuries when he slipped into a code blue. He was revived and placed on a ventilator to help with breathing. Jimmy was taken into surgery to remove the dead burns of skin from his body with a process called debridement. Then his wounds were covered with cool dressings. Jimmy's body was covered in gauze, and he was heavily sedated to relieve his agonizing pain. Jimmy's state was critical, and the next forty-eight hours would be crucial.

Meanwhile, Glo and Keith were treated for trauma and minor cuts. Glo was completely stunned over the painful vision that danced in her mind. It was less than twelve hours ago that she put her babies to sleep and the reality that she would never see their beautiful faces again had not yet sunk in. Glo sat motionless as if the impact of the episode had knocked the air from her lungs. She was also scared about the dire condition that her husband was in and didn't know if she would lose him as well. Keith was speechless as he desperately tried to make sense of it all.

Glo was eventually questioned by members of the fire and police departments, despite her grief-stricken state. They totally sympathized with her, but it was imperative to get an account of what transpired while the events were still fresh in her mind. Her statement cited that the fire originated from Louis's room. He had apparently fallen asleep while smoking a cigarette and ignited the mattress. He obviously panicked, along with being inebriated, and dragged the burning innerspring into the bathtub. He closed the door, and Glo was awakened by the scent of smoke. Glo said once she and Jimmy were made aware of Louis's actions that everything from that point on played out like a terrible nightmare. Glo informed the officials that she was forced outside to summons help and the next thing she witnessed were flames moving through her home at a rapid speed. She then heard an explosion and Jimmy's burning body came flying out the second-floor window. Shortly afterwards, they spotted Keith and waved him over to join them.

Glo added a significant piece of information to the story and that was Louis had started a minor fire a week prior. He had obviously come home from a drinking escapade and dropped a lit cigarette on a pile of socks. There was no damage that occurred and there was no way that she believed he would be so careless only a week later. Afterward, when Jimmy was strong enough to give a statement, it would be consistent with the one Glo made.

Meanwhile, in front of the place that was once the Alfords' peaceful dwelling, the fire officials faced the grim task of carrying the blanket-wrapped bodies of the young victims out of the building. The charred bodies of the children were located on the second floor, and the two youngest kids were discovered huddled next to Louis's corpse. It was a dreadful sight, despite officials seeing catastrophes on a regular basis. The actuality of losing seven children in such a disaster at once brought on complete despair.

Mount Sinai Hospital on Chicago's West Side quickly filled with family, friends, and colleagues once the news of the unfortunate incident traveled throughout the city. Jimmy's department immediately reacted to the incident. Sergeant O'Grady and Commander Earl Johnson were among the many who rushed to Jimmy's side. Commander Johnson was named to head five trustees of the fund that was organized in Jimmy's behalf. It was endorsed by the superintendent, Orlando Wilson at the time, and it began immediately. The police department was supplied envelopes to be returned to Cosmopolitan Bank of Chicago, located on 801 N. Clark, and private citizens' contributions were also welcomed.

It was difficult for Jimmy's superiors to see him in such a feeble state. They sympathized with the human element of the disaster, but they felt a greater sorrow, since this tragedy occurred to one of their own. Sergeant O'Grady felt that it was an absolute tragedy and for Jimmy to be unsuccessful in his heroic effort to save his children was heartbreaking, to say the least. They left not knowing if Jimmy would survive the ordeal, but they also knew there was work that had to be done in order to assist their fellow officer for what was best for him and his family. The police chaplain, Father McPolin, arrived at the hospital to provide comfort for the grieving parents. Jimmy was in and out of consciousness, his eyes fluttering, as he whispered to Father McPolin that they didn't deserve this fatality and he wanted him to give his children a blessing. Jimmy was enduring physical, mental, and emotional pain, all wrapped into one. Glo didn't want to leave Jimmy's side, but she had to get a breather, just to keep her sanity.

The Friday morning editions of the Chicago newspapers were flooded with the Alfords' horrific tragedy. It was the first story broadcasted on every news station, and media outlets played the story throughout the day. It was even featured in the *Birmingham Post,* Birmingham being the place where Jimmy was born. Although a racial undertone was used, as they referred to Jimmy as "the Husky Negro," the majority of the people realized that the anguish the Alfords were enduring had no color attached to it. It was a heartfelt topic that touched the essence of people of all races, and parents cringed over the unthinkable. To lose one child was extremely heartbreaking, but to have seven snatched away in a blink of an eye seemed unimaginable. The reports from the media outlets were pretty much consistent, with only a few variations in the story.

The one fact that was undisputable was that the fire was indeed started by Louis Robinson. Glo and Keith were provided shelter by a family member. Glo quietly sat by Jimmy's bedside, not knowing if Jimmy would encounter the same fate that took her precious children away. Jimmy had slipped into a code blue a couple of more times and had to be revived. Glo knew nothing could prepare her for the pain of losing her soul mate, along with her seven children. She had loved Jimmy their entire union, without boundaries, and devoted her entire life to him. Their foundation was filled with love, laughter, and wonderful memories. Glo helplessly watched her husband's face in agony, and it seemed unreachable to soothe. Jimmy's pain was immense, as his breaths came in ragged shallow gasps, with his lungs struggling. The strong solid man of many words who had always beaten the odds seemed to be slipping away.

The outpouring of love and support for the Alfords was overwhelming and greatly appreciated. Jimmy's hospital room stayed crowded with visitors who wanted to give him the will to keep fighting and not give up. As Glo struggled with the idea of delaying the funeral just in case Jimmy didn't survive, the department went to bat for Jimmy in another way. When the horrific incident occurred, the Chief of Detectives felt that Jimmy should not be considered injured in the line of duty. Sergeant O'Grady knew that would ultimately affect how Jimmy's hospital bills were paid, and if he passed away, it would be under a different circumstance than an accidental death. However, if he was considered injured in the line of duty, Glo would receive half of Jimmy's pay for the rest of his life, and his survivors would receive benefits.

O'Grady immediately tried to convince the First Deputy Superintendent, James Rochford, that Jimmy's tragedy should be considered as an officer injured in the line of duty. It took a lot of back and forth, but it was finally declared by Superintendent Orlando Wilson as an injury in the line of duty. O'Grady knew besides the tragedy that there were practicalities that needed to be taken into consideration. He did what he thought was best and had it resolved in the most beneficial way for James and his family. The bomb and arson department immediately launched an investigation. They looked at the site closely to see if the fire was set on purpose, but nothing was discovered suspicious, as they concluded their investigation.

Finally, Glo decided, with the support of the family members, that it was time to plan a proper burial for her children. She would lean on her strong faith in God to restore Jimmy's strength enough for him to eventually recover. Although Glo knew life for her would never be the same, it would be more tolerable to have her husband by her side. Glo made her decision that A.R. Leak Funeral Home would handle her children's funeral arrangements. The funeral home had established itself in Chicago with a vision from A.R. Leak to help African Americans bury their loved ones in a respectful manner. Their policy from day one of opening their doors had always been to give individuals a proper send-off, even if families didn't have the resources to pay for a funeral. Their business started on 45th and State, where blacks resided. The Leak family was reluctant to relocate to the Chatham area, which at the time, was mostly white. It was a risky move, because there was a strong possibility of them losing a lot of potential clients. Nevertheless, they took a chance and decided to break a barrier that restricted blacks from being welcomed in certain areas of Chicago.

Mr. A.R. Leak was very involved in the civil rights movement and was great friends with Dr. M. L. King. The Leak Funeral Home was located across the street from a well-known restaurant that at the time was segregated. A.R. Leak became the first African American to dine at the restaurant. When the Leaks moved on Cottage Grove, they held an open house to introduce their new business to the neighborhood. People came from everywhere to show their support for A.R. Leak by gathering en mass in the parking lot on that Sunday afternoon. But the following day, on Monday, no one called to acquire their services. The next couple of weeks came around and still the Leaks had not acquired any business. It could have been a discouraging period for them, but their strong belief that their business was founded by God kept them motivated and hopeful.

After a month, the expenses mounted up and still they hadn't received a first call. Finally, a woman walked through the door, seeking their services, after the untimely death of her daughter, who was only in her twenties at the time of her demise. After sitting down with A.R. Leak, it was revealed that the lady didn't have one single dollar to pay for funeral expenses. Leak sympathized with the lady, as he did with all his clients. He excused himself and went to speak with the rest of his family regarding this matter. He simply looked at his boys and said, "Boys, this is our first customer in our new location. She has no money and I think we should give her a funeral at no cost, but not just any ordinary funeral. Let's give her one fit for a princess."

The Leaks agreed and placed the beautiful young lady in an expensive casket. They did everything required to have a funeral that represented class and dignity. The Leaks were extremely grateful to finally have a client, and that generosity became what they were known for across the city. To this very day, they have financially assisted many families by providing free funerals and burials for their loved ones. A.R. Leak had another obstacle to tackle being in the funeral business. It was when a mother wanted her daughter buried in Chicago Oakwood Cemetery. During this time, it was an all-white cemetery, despite it being located in a mostly black neighborhood.

The cemetery refused to bury the remains of the young lady among the whites buried there.

A.R. Leak organized a march, along with Rev. Clay Evans, other well-known ministers, and the NAACP, from the funeral home on Cottage Grove to Oakwood Cemetery, to change its policy and open its gates to African Americans. This was yet another milestone where the Leaks' involvement helped to change the course of history for blacks in the city of Chicago. O'Grady, knowing the strong character of A.R. Leak and his family, didn't hesitate to call on him and ask for his assistance in burying the Alford children. There were a few fundraisers in place to generate funds, but no one wanted to continue to delay the inevitable painful goodbyes to the Alford children.

It was confirmed that the Leak family would render their services at no cost. O'Grady and Johnson would also correlate the response of the police department for the funeral and aftermath. When Glo walked into the funeral home to finalize the arrangements, Spencer Leak Sr. marveled over her strength. He witnessed a petite woman with remarkable courage who even found a way to muster and keep a gracious smile through her agony. Mr. Leak had witnessed many mothers completely unhinged having to bury one of their children, and she had lost seven of her offspring all at once, not to mention the reality that her husband's life was hanging by a thread. The Leaks knew it was the most difficult and unforeseen task that Glo ever faced. The entire police department and city of Chicago were grieving right along with her. She finalized the arrangements and prepared for a day that would be etched in her memory for the rest of her life.

The sun shined brightly on the morning of February 25th, 1964. The unusual 40-degree weather, in one of the coldest winter months of Chicago, symbolized the sparkling imprint the Alford children were leaving behind. The front of A.R. Leak Funeral Home was filled with mourners waiting to pay their last respects. People lined up for blocks to extend their condolences to a family left with an emptiness that could never be filled. It was evident by the outpouring of folks present that this tragedy had a major impact on the city of Chicago. This was the first catastrophe of this magnitude, to lose seven children all at once, in such a horrific incident. The Andrews family was among the people grief-stricken by the horrific event. Although they were no longer neighbors, the Andrews still considered the Alfords like family. It was extremely difficult for them (especially MaDear) to deal with the reality that such precious young lives had been snatched away by such a senseless and negligent incident.

The police department flooded the streets to direct traffic and keep things moving in an orderly manner. The mood surrounding the funeral home was complete sadness as people stepped out of their vehicles. People were devastated to the core of their souls and wanted to express love to the grieving family. Inside the funeral home, there were seven white-velvet-lined caskets with the children's pictures on top. Unable to fathom the reality occurring right before her eyes, Glo began to sob uncontrollably, desperately calling out for her babies. With Spencer Leak Sr. and Jimmy's partner by her side, her knees were buckling, and she was no longer able to stand, and the two were there to catch her fall. It was a helpless sight that stayed in the consciousness of many, no matter how much they tried to erase it.

In the front pew, Glo, Keith, and Lovejoy (Jimmy's mother) sat in silent grief, awaiting the start of the funeral service. At the designated hour to start the service, Jimmy lay in his hospital bed, suffering from a broken leg and severe burns, bearing his grief in lonely silence. Prayers were read, tributes were made, and the eulogy was given by the Rev. William Bertha of the Harvey Community Church. He spoke words of encouragement to Glo and reminded her that as long as her children lived in her heart they would live on. Beautiful hymns were played in remembrance of the hearts the Alford children touched in such a brief but meaningful time. People could only shake their heads in disbelief as they extended their condolences to the family before departing.

The forty-two pallbearers, all from the Chicago Police Department, marched the tiny coffins to the hearses that lined up outside the funeral home. Mr. Spencer Leak Sr., along with others who worked at the Leak Funeral Home, assisted with loading the coffins into the vehicles. It was time for the Alford children to be transported to their final resting place. The procession extended for blocks en route to Lincoln Cemetery, located at 12300 S. Kedzie Avenue.

The sun had melted the snow at the cemetery and forced the pallbearers to step around patches of mud as they moved the seven tiny coffins to the gravesite. The mourners walked with their heads bowed down as they gathered around for the final farewell. The grief Glo carried inside of her tore at her like a tornado, as the tiny coffins were lowered into the ground. The fact that she would never see their beautiful faces or feel their warm embrace again totally devastated her. As Glo started to go down with her children, Spencer Leak Sr. had to once again catch her fall, as the grief overcame her.

The sight of the caskets going into the ground also was too much for Keith to handle. For the first time since the incident, he allowed himself to express his pain, as he yelled out, "All the little brothers and sisters!"

It was evident, as people departed the burial grounds, that this devastating incident would have a lingering effect for many years to come. As Glo and Keith held each other up and reluctantly walked away from the burial ground, they knew a part of their souls were buried along with the children.

James E. Alford 10mths

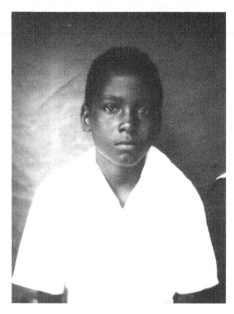

James E. Alford As A Young Boy

James and Brother Billy

A Young Love Mr. and Mrs. James E. Alford

James With 1st Born Keith

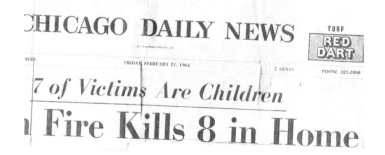

News Paper Article

Headlines Next Day

Firemen fight blaze in the home of Detective James Alford, 4136 W. Gladys, where seven of the eight Alford children lost their lives early Friday. Smoke still pours from the attic of the house where the bodies of the youngsters were found. (Photo by Joseph Marino)

Fighting The Fire

GRIM REMINDERS OF A TRAGEDY— A crushed plastic baby bottle and a child's charred shoe found in the living room of the James Alford home, 4136 Gladys, serve as grim reminders to Fillmore Ptlmn. Arthur Foster of the tragic fire that claimed the lives of seven of the Alford's eight children. A cousin living with the family also perished.

Policeman Finds Charred Baby Bottle& Shoe

8 BLAMED ON SMOKING IN BED

7 Children of Cop Die with Relative

A fire which swept the home of a Chicago policeman early yesterday, killing seven of his eight children, was blamed by police on a relative's smoking in bed.

The relative, L. T. Robinson, 51, who rented a bedroom in the bungalow at 4136 Gladys av., also perished in the children's attic bedroom as he tried to save them. The father, Detective James Alford, 37, was burned seriously as he also sought to rescue them. He tumbled thru a second floor window to the front lawn, his clothing aflame. Robinson was Seford's cousin.

Boy, 14, Escapes

The dead children were James Jr., 11; Denise, 9; Calvin, 8; Patricia, 6; Tyrone, 4; Steve, 5; and Christine, 1. Their brother, Keith, 14, jumped from a window of the attic bedroom and was unhurt.

Arthur Siebert, chief of the 23d battalion, gave this account of the blaze:

The mattress in Robinson's bed burst into flames at about 2 a. m. Robinson dragged the mattress from the bedroom into a bathroom and stuffed it into a bathtub.

Fire and Smoke Spread

He shut the bathroom door and called to Alford, who ran from his bedroom to find flames spreading in the bedroom and bathroom and the home filling with smoke.

Keith told investigators he was awakened by his mother's screams and roused his brothers and sisters. He said he started to lead them down the stairs, but they were forced back by the flames.

Alford and Robinson ran thru the fire to try to save the children. Mrs. Alford remained downstairs and sought to summon the fire department. The phone wires, however, had been burned, and the phone was useless. She ran outside.

Draft Spurs Flames

Upstairs, Alford opened a window to the attic bedroom—the one thru which Keith later jumped. After the window was open, a draft sucked up flames and smoke with a noise that neighbors said sounded like a minor explosion. In moments,

[TRIBUNE Staff Photos]
Ruins of bungalow at 4136 Gladys av. in which eight persons perished when flames spread rapidly. Seven victims were children of Detective James Alford.

Father Pat McPolin, police chaplain, talking with James Alford in Mount Sinai hospital.

the bedroom became an inferno.

Soon after Keith had jumped, Alford fell out of a second window. He was lying on the lawn, near his wife's feet, when firemen arrived. He was taken to Mount Sinai hospital with second and third degree burns on the arms, head, and body. He was reported in serious condition.

The bodies of Robinson and the children were found, badly burned, on the floor of the attic room. Keith said that, when he jumped from the window, he had expected the others to follow him. None did.

Family Dog Destroyed

A final victim was the family's dog, Gaylord. The dog fled from the building with his fur aflame and had to be destroyed by a policeman.

Mrs. Alford told police that Robinson had been drinking heavily thru the day and evening. She said a minor fire

Firemen removing one of eight bodies from fire-stricken home.

broke out in his room a week ago, when he dropped a lighted cigaret in a pile of socks after drinking.

Fellow officers of Alford in the Maxwell Street robbery detail organized a fund drive to assist the family. Earl Johnson, commander of the robbery detail, was named to head five trustees for the fund.

Alford had been a policeman since 1954. He was described by Johnson as a "highly regarded officer."

Mrs. Alford and Keith were staying yesterday with her sister, Mrs. Mayvis Washington, 541 W. 57th pl.

Damage from the fire was estimated at $5,000.

Night Of Fire

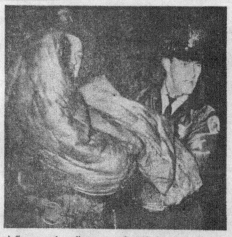

7 CHILDREN

A family friend comforts Keith Alford, 13, survivor of fire that killed his seven brothers and sisters early Friday. The blaze that swept the family bungalow at 4136 W. Gladys also injured his father, Detective James Alford, and his mother, Gloria. A cousin of the Alfords was also killed.

A fireman and a policeman carry out blanket-wrapped body of one of the young fire victims.

Family Consoles Surviving Child As Firemen Carry
Deceased Children Bodies Wrapped In Blankets

James E. Alford Jr. 11-12-52

Denise Marlene Alford 1-14-55

Kelvin Tommy Alford 3-23-56

Patricia Diane Alford 3-3-57

Steven Brian Alford 12-01-58

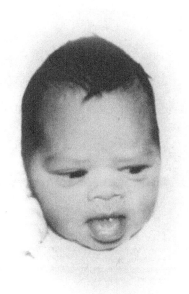

Tyrone Phillip Alford 11-16-60

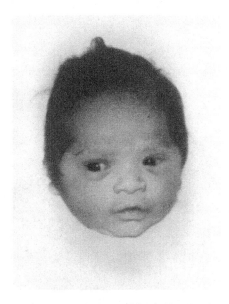

Christine Renae Alford 12-17-62

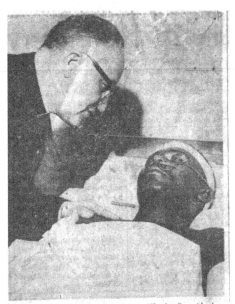

At Mount Sinai Hospital, Det. James Alford talks with the Rev. Patrick McPolin, police department chaplain. Alford was injured and burned in attempting to save his children from blazing West Side home. (AP)

Visitors Pray For James

Tormented: Sight of her seven children in caskets at Chicago funeral nearly tore the heart out of Mrs. James Alford, whose detective husband at that moment lay near death at hospital suffering injuries received in unsuccessfully trying to rescue the kids from the flaming inferno.

Spencer Leak Sr. Assists Mrs. Alford During Funeral

Det. Alford missed the mass funeral for his seven children because he was not far from death himself at local hospital.

Chicago Lawman Misses Funeral For His 7 Children

At the designated hour of the funeral for his seven children, Chicago detective James Alford, 37, had to bear his grief in lonely silence as he lay in a hospital suffering with a broken leg and severe burns all over his body, sustained in his determined, but unsuccessful attempt to rescue his seven children from the tragic, raging fire that destroyed the family's home. Grieved detectives from the city's robbery units acted as pallbearers for the children of their fellow officer, and Alford's wife, Gloria, 35, and their surviving child, Keith, 14, attended the sad last rites.

James In Hospital Unable To Attend His Childrens Funeral

DNESDAY, FEBRUARY 26, 19

7 TINY COFFINS LAID TO REST IN SNOWY FIELD

BY THOMAS FITZPATRICK

The sun gleamed so brightly yesterday that the snow at Lincoln cemetery was melting underfoot.

The 42 pallbearers, all members of the Chicago police department, stepped around patches of mud as they bore the seven tiny white coffins to the graveside.

All seven of the children—four boys and three girls, ranging in age from eleven to one—died Friday in a fire at their home at 4136 Gladys av.

Father in Hospital

Detective James E. Alford, 37, their father, wasn't able to attend the services. He was still in Mount Sinai hospital being treated for burns and a broken leg suffered when he attempted to save the children.

Mrs. Alford was there and she listened impassively to the funeral sermon given by the Rev. William A. Bertha of the Harvey Memorial Community church.

The Rev. Mr. Bertha spoke of the trials of Job and said that as long as the seven children were carried in the hearfs of their mother and father they were still alive.

Only One Child Left

Mrs. Alford's son, Keith, 14, was at her side. He was the only child left now of a family that just days ago had included James Jr., 11; Denise, 9; Calvin, 8; Patricia, 6; Steve, 5; Tyrone, 4; and Christine 1.

Keith was with his brothers and sisters when the fire broke out in their attic sleeping quarters. He tried to take the two smallest and drop them out the window, but Leroy T. Robinson, 51, his father's cousin, had grabbed them, promising that he would save them.

The bodies of two children were found huddled near Robinson's body several hours later. The fire had started in Robinson's bed, firemen said, after he fell asleep while smoking.

"I'll Try to Be Brave"

"I'll try to be brave," Mrs Alford told the Rev. Mr. Berth yesterday before the 50 ca caravan left the funeral chape at 7838 Cottage Grove av.

The sight of the seven whit coffins at graveside proved to

BURY 7 FIRE VICTIMS

Seven stark white caskets, mute evidence of a fire tragedy which struck the home of Detective James Alford of 4136 Gladys ave, last week, are borne to waiting hearses (there are shown here) for the trip to the cemetery following rites at A. R. Leak Funeral chapel. Pallbearers are members of Chicago Police force who are co-workers of Alford.

MOURN GREAT LOSS

Mrs. Gloria Alford, right, and her son, Keith register grief as they leave A. R. Leak Funeral Chapel following rites for seven children of the family, whose lives were snuffed out in a flash fire last wek. The father, James, is still hospitalized from the holocaust.—Rhoden photo.

Page 23 · DAILY DEFENDER — WEDNESDAY, FEBRUARY 26.

Day of Funeral

Article Day of Service

Pictures of Children

Keith and James Jr.

Children Photo's

Chicago

FRIDAY, FEBRUARY 21, 1964

7 CHILDREN KILLED IN FIRE

Seven of the eight children of Chicago Detective James E. Alford perished in a fire that destroyed their home at 4136 Gladys Avenue, Chicago, Illinois. The children, James, Jr., 11; Denise, 9; Kelvin, 8; Patricia, 6; Steve, 5; Tyrone, 4; and Christine, 1; were all trapped in second floor bedrooms.

Mr. Alford was severely burned while risking his life in an attempt to save the children.

Mr. Alford's family policy was issued February 1, 1964 by the Commonwealth Life and Accident Insurance Company. The fire occurred 20 days later. $7,000.00 in death benefits was promptly paid.

The Commonwealth Life and Accident Insurance Company was proud to have covered the Alford Family and to be of assistance to them at the time of this tragedy.

Chicago, Illinois

March 30, 1964

Commonwealth Life and Accident Insurance Company
Attention Claim Department
2400 West Madison Street
Chicago, Illinois

Dear Mr. Dash:

I am writing you in my hour of grief because I am so thankful to your fine company. As you know, I just buried my seven small children, ages from one to eleven, who all died in a fire on February 21, 1964. I took the policy with your company February 1, 1964 and made one payment and the policy paid immediate full benefit. I was only in the insurance twenty days. The money helped me to give the children a respectable Christian funeral. The personal attention and consideration given me will always be remembered.

I most certainly will always recommend your fine Commonwealth Insurance Company to everyone. You may use my name and this letter in your advertising in explaining your insurance to other people.

God bless you all.

James E. Alford Sr.
Gloria Alford.

Article Of Letter To Insurance Company

THE BULLETIN, THURSDAY, APRIL 23, 1964

Englewood Clergy Aids Fire Victim

FROM the Civic Liberty League of Illinois calls on Alford in his room Sinai hospital to show him check donated in the James Alford Children's fund, seven of his eight children who lost their lives (left to right) are Rev. ... , 7559 S. Aberdeen, Leaguer Delcoessie Freeman, ... pastor, New Friendship Missionary Baptist church, 844 W. 71st st. Rev. Edmond Blair, pastor, Omega Baptist church and Rev. William L. Lambert, Greater Mt. Hope Baptist church, 5636 Normal, Leaguer said donations to the fund, initiated by the League, are still being accepted at the headquarters of the organization, 7838 S. Cottage Grove ave. Alford, who was seriously burned, his wife and one son survived the tragic fire.

A.R. Leak and Members of The Civic Liberty League

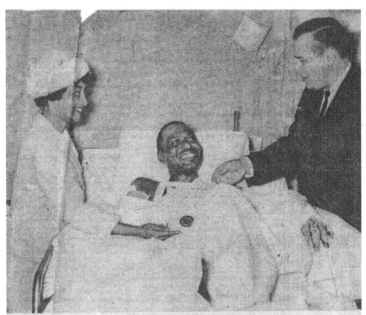

CHICAGO'S HERO POLICEMAN

Lt. Earl Johnson, Commander of the Detective Division Robbery Section, presents Det. James Alford, Area Four Robbery, with award for outstanding police work, at Mt. Sinai Hospital, as his wife, Gloria, looks on. The awards are usually made in area headquarters, but since Alford, seriously burned when fire ravaged his home last Feb. 21, was still hospitalized, a bedside ceremony was made. The honoree lost seven of his eight children in the fire. Det. Alford, 37, and five other detectives received citations for their outstanding work in connection with the arrests of a gang of seven robbers who had committed 75 robberies, killing two persons. The Alfords live at 4136 W. Gladys Ave.

CHICAGO'S HERO POLICEMAN

Former Superintendant James O'Grady

Spencer Leak, Sr. President, Leak & Sons Funeral Home

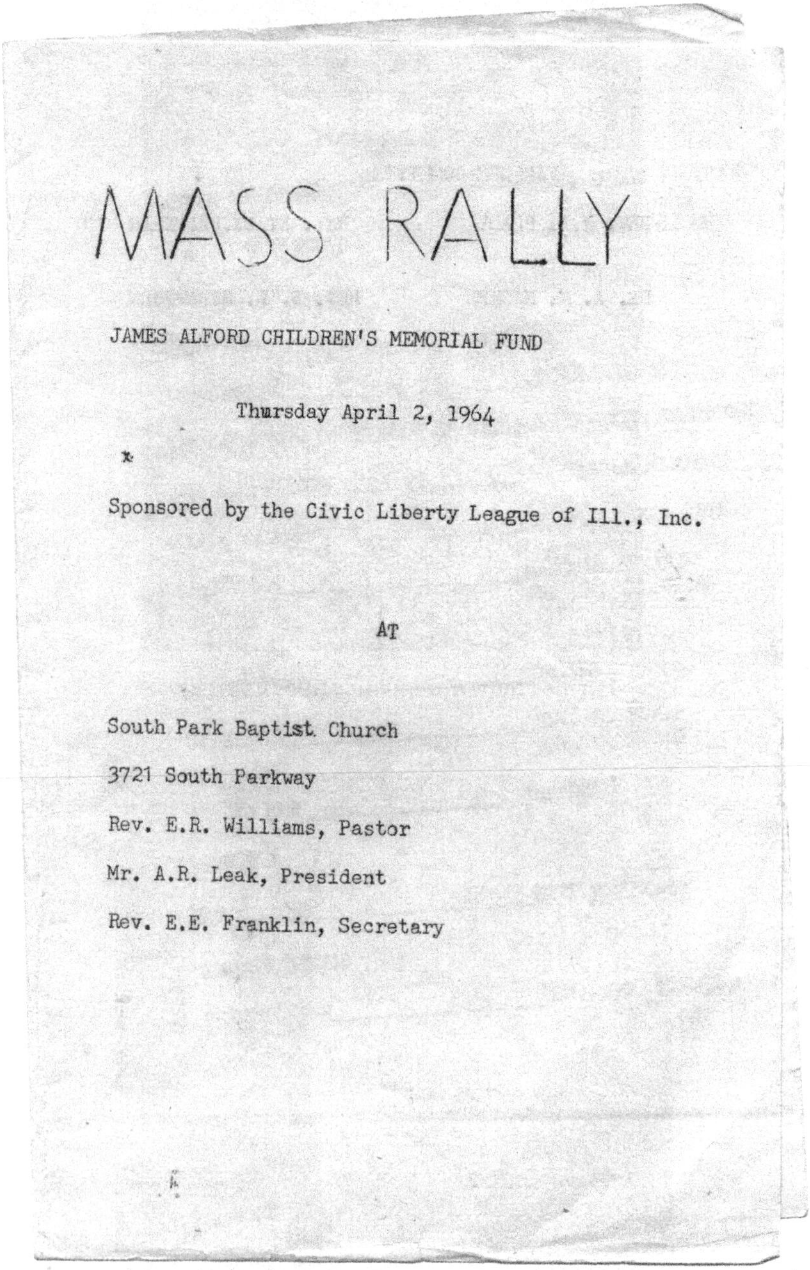

MASS RALLY

JAMES ALFORD CHILDREN'S MEMORIAL FUND

Thursday April 2, 1964

Sponsored by the Civic Liberty League of Ill., Inc.

AT

South Park Baptist Church

3721 South Parkway

Rev. E.R. Williams, Pastor

Mr. A.R. Leak, President

Rev. E.E. Franklin, Secretary

Mass Rally Fundraiser

AN EVERLASTING FLAME

The flames from the Alfords' tragedy claimed lives, but also united a city during a very challenging time. The severity of the losses was still in Glo's limbs as much as on her mind. The only consolation to soothe her suffering was the knowledge that her children were safe in God's arms. Glo still had to contend with the major hurdle that lingered on her heart, and that was Jimmy's dire condition. The wish for her husband to be by her side during this difficult time appeared to be an unreachable aspiration. She had been forced to reveal a strength that had been concealed deeply in her soul until now. Jimmy had always been depended on to assure her that everything was going to be okay, but he was now fighting for his life. If it hadn't been for the city of Chicago embracing the Alford family in their time of need, Glo could have easily slipped into a deep depression.

The Alfords lost everything in the fire. Although personal possessions had little value, compared to the lives lost, monetary assistance was still needed to help the Alfords pick up the pieces and move on. Fundraisers began to be held across the city after the initial fund was set up by the department. The Garfield Family Council collected money for the Alford family in a fundraiser led by the president, Rev. Joseph Kelly. The neighbors of the

Alfords requested the council to be trustees of a fund. The Garfield Park Chamber of Commerce was also involved in raising revenue. They served as an advocate for businesses and residents of the Garfield Park area, the neighborhood the Alfords resided in before the fire. The Cosmopolitan National Bank, located on Chicago Avenue, set up a memorial fund, called The Children of Detective James Alford Memorial Fund. The citizens of Chicago were directed to make their contributions as well. The Chicago press photographers voted to donate to the Alford family and their generous gesture was greatly appreciated.

The local churches were also instrumental in assisting the Alfords: New Friendship Missionary Baptist Church, Mt. Hope Baptist Church, and Omega Baptist Church, just to name a few. The city came together and displayed a tremendous amount of support. It didn't matter the gender or race, as everyone sympathized with the shocking chain of events that shattered the Alfords' world. The racial tension that was still an issue seemed to dissolve during that inconceivable time. It was a time of deep mourning because parents still imagined the emptiness that no amount of time could fill.

As the donations poured in, Jimmy remained hospitalized in critical condition. The prayers for his recovery came from everywhere and visitors continued to surround his bedside in support. The surgeons had performed skin grafts on Jimmy and he was always heavily sedated to subdue his pain. They kept his body bandaged because his skin was sensitive to the touch. His chest, back, and arms had endured the most damage. He also lay in bed with his leg in traction from the broken leg he suffered from the second-floor fall. It was heartbreaking to visit Jimmy in the state he was in, but Glo remained by his bedside. The doctors had expressed to Glo that Jimmy was still not out of the woods, and if he recovered, it would be a long process.

By April 2nd, 1964, the lingering effects of the tragedy were still fresh in everyone's mind. The Civil Liberty League of Illinois sponsored a mass rally for The James Alford Children's Memorial Fund. People were still committed to offering their time and financial assistance to help the Alfords in any way possible. The event was held at the South Park Baptist Church and orchestrated by the Rev. E. R. Williams and Mr. A.R. Leak. Local choirs performed, but the featured vocal group was The Staples Singers, most known for their hit song, "Let's Do It Again." It was a song written by Curtis Mayfield that was part of the soundtrack for the successful movie starring

Bill Cosby and Curtis Mayfield. In addition, Mr. A.R. Leak presented the state of purpose and an offering was taken in behalf of the Alfords.

Another overwhelming expression of generosity came from Commonwealth Life Insurance. The Alfords' family policy was issued on February 1st, 1964, and the fire occurred three weeks later. They had only made one payment to the company, but the policy paid full benefits. They were proud to have assisted the Alford family at this time of tragedy. A few of the checks raised from the donations were presented to Glo in Jimmy's hospital room. It gave Jimmy a feeling of solace to see that the citizens of Chicago sympathized with what his family was going through and knowing that his family wasn't suffering this hardship alone.

Jimmy continued his long journey toward recovery from his near-fatal experience. The visitors continued to visit Jimmy in the hospital and spoke words of encouragement for his complete healing. The strong bonds that were being created across the city from the Alfords' misfortune were enormous. The department continued their undying support for one of their own. It didn't lessen the Alfords' pain of suffering such a traumatic loss. But it was gratifying for them to know that a shimmer of hope came from such a tragedy. The united effort, to help a family in need, which came from the city, was incredible.

Sergeant O'Grady stated, "There was no one who thought, oh, those are just black kids. Although there were some terrible things going on in the country, that thought was erased when this disaster hit Jimmy's doorstep."

Jimmy was looked upon as a hero who acted without hesitation to save his children. O'Grady's and the rest of the department's hearts went out to Jimmy, having that amount of courage to risk his own life for his children.

The long fight for equality finally culminated in the Civil Rights Act enacted on July 2nd, 1964, which ended segregation in public places and banned employment discrimination on the basis of race, color, religion, sex, or national origin. It was a celebration for African Americans across the country to have a law passed that prohibited racial discrimination.

Time passed and although the Alfords' tragedy may have faded away in the media, it didn't in the hearts of many. That time marked a period in Chicago that became a part of the city's history. While Jimmy was still recuperating in the hospital, he was presented a citation from Commander Earl Johnson and Sergeant O'Grady for outstanding police work. He led an investigation that led to the arrest of a gang of seven robbers who had committed seventy-five robberies. After months of intense medical attention, Jimmy was finally released from the hospital. The permanent scars that he would carry for the rest of his life would never outweigh that which turned his world upside down. He still managed to smile through distress and never complained. His physical therapy continued to build his strength, and Jimmy wasn't ashamed of the visible scars permanently left on his body.

Jimmy was eventually awarded by the department for his heroic effort and was also presented a memorial fund check. By the time Jimmy was strong enough to return to work, O'Grady had moved to the vice control section. There, he focused on organized gambling and prostitution rackets. O'Grady had a couple of close death encounters himself, one being shot in the hip, while chasing a purse snatcher in the loop, and on another occasion, wrestling with four Chinese men who were accused of extorting money from Chinese American restaurateurs. Still, O'Grady was perceived by his peers and subordinates as a "new-style" educated cop. He considered Jimmy's heroic efforts to save his family among the bravest he had ever witnessed. O'Grady was overjoyed that Jimmy had fought his way back and got what he deserved, which was injured in the line of duty.

Jimmy's unfortunate circumstances became one of the catalysts for a former superintendent, who later helped form an organization known today as the Chicago Police Memorial Foundation. It generates millions of dollars to set aside to provide support and financial assistance to families of Chicago police officers killed or injured in the line of duty. When Spencer Leak Sr. finally saw Jimmy's wounds, like most, he wondered how he survived. Spencer Sr. felt Jimmy was an incredible man to have endured that type of pain and lose his entire family. But Jimmy lived his life according to the rule that what doesn't kill you only makes you stronger. He would find a way to dig deeply into his soul and not surrender to a life of regrets and despair.

Jimmy and Keith suppressed the tragic night and rarely discussed it, while Glo accepted that things would never be the same for their family because too much was lost. She also shared a couple of safety precautions with the city of Chicago about fire prevention, one being that people who have attic rooms shouldn't allow kids to sleep in them because smoke and fire move upward. And attics can become a fire trap. The next warning, which Glo was adamant about, was, never smoke in bed!

Relationships continued to blossom from the Alfords' dark season that brought some much needed togetherness in the city. O'Grady and Spencer Sr.'s bond resulted in O'Grady later appointing him as Director of Cook County Jail when he became Cook County Sheriff. Although Leak's credentials and resume were adequate to land the position on his own merit, the relationship he and O'Grady developed from the Alfords' incident made the appointment that much greater. The fantastic manner in which Leak Funeral Home handled the services for the Alford children gained them visible notoriety.

At the end of the year, people lined up for blocks in front of Leak Funeral Home to view the body of legendary singer, Sam Cooke. Cooke was killed in Los Angeles, but most of his family lived in the Chatham area of Chicago. His parents asked his wife to allow his body to be flown back to Chicago for a wake and funeral. It was held in the same chapel where the Alford children had their funeral. However, something wonderful occurred during this difficult and painful time, which was the bond that developed between the Alfords and the Leaks, which would carry on for generations to come!

The Alfords knew that no matter how difficult it seemed life must go on. They were able to put a down payment on a bi-level home with the memorial fund collected by Jimmy's fellow police officers. As they looked forward to new beginnings, the Alfords' seven deceased children would be cherished in their hearts forever!

THE AFTERMATH: NEW BEGINNINGS

The Alfords finally settled in their new eight-room bi-level home, located at 101 S. Princeton Avenue, with hopes of new beginnings. It was a difficult transition because once again they were faced with a dilemma to overcome. During the time their new home was being built, it was set on fire three times, forcing the builders to start over each time. The neighborhood was predominantly white and they didn't want the Alfords there. It was unimaginable that people would be so heartless and cruel knowing the family had just suffered a traumatic loss from a fire. Even though the majority of people didn't see color when it came to what the Alfords went through, a few were consumed by hatred, allowing their racism to override any humane or compassionate feelings they may have had.

When the Alfords were able to move into their new home, it was obvious that they were not welcomed. Keith had trouble with the white boys in the neighborhood to the extent that his father had to come to the rescue a few times. Jimmy had called his fellow officers out on a couple of occasions to report a disturbance, but it didn't seem to alter anything. One day, Jimmy decided to take matters into his own hands. He was sitting on the front porch, cleaning his gun, when a few white folks approached and observed him for a moment before asking, "Are you a cop?" Jimmy looked dead in their eyes and said, "If I'm not then somebody's in trouble!" They backed up and knew to stay away from the Alford family.

Soon, it came to the point where there was white flight in the neighborhood. The white neighbors began packing up their belongings and moving away. Once again, life went on for the Alfords, and in order to live with the haunting memories of the tragedy, they suppressed their sadness and continued on with their lives with as much normality as possible.

The one-year anniversary of the children's death also marked another setback for the black race when Muslim minister and human rights activist, Malcolm X, was assassinated. He was shot by Nation of Islam members while addressing a crowd at a rally in New York City. Malcolm X did not share Martin Luther King's belief regarding nonviolence. He believed that African Americans should defend themselves by any means necessary. Although Malcolm's views may have not promoted peace when confronted by the oppressor, he is still considered an influential leader in African American history.

The children's unexpected deaths left a silence that diminished Glo's hope for a brighter tomorrow. She was accustomed to a house filled with laughter, noise, and the chatter of children throughout the day. Now her days were filled with lonely hours of trying to make it through the day. The surviving son, Keith, was now in high school and entering a stage of independence and early manhood. Glo could have easily allowed her grief to swallow every part of her until she would be too numb to feel the pain of such devastating loss.

Instead, as things turned out, Jimmy and Glo welcomed their ninth child on June 19th, 1965. Their son, Darryl Alford, was truly a blessing, bringing joy and happiness back into the Alfords' life. Nevertheless, Glo couldn't help but think of the children she lost when she looked at Darryl's small, innocent face. It was an incident that would forever remain etched in her mind and soul, making her shiver each time she thought about that unforgettable night.

The Chicago Campaign began in July of that same year when local civil rights groups invited Dr. King to lead demonstrations against segregation in education and housing and employment discrimination. Although the Civil

Rights Act of 1964 outlawed segregation, it did not end discrimination, as blacks continued to be kept out of a vast majority of white middle-class neighborhoods. The movement was also led by Chicago activist, Albert Raby, who was the leader of the Coordinating Council of Community Organizations. It was their hope that the campaign would be successful in allowing blacks into neighborhoods that offered better education opportunities and greater jobs. The Southern Christian Leadership Conference also joined in, launching Operation Breadbasket. They appointed a young twenty-five-year-old Rev. Jesse Jackson to organize a campaign that targeted companies and corporations that refused to hire blacks. This intense campaign gained recognition through demonstrations, boycotts, and marches.

It was during that time that Mr. Spencer Leak Sr. chauffeured Dr. King around the city of Chicago. He was responsible for driving him to Soldier Field, where he delivered his speech on the housing crisis that blacks faced in Chicago. Dr. King wanted the nation to see firsthand the conditions that black people were forced to live in, compared to the white people on the North Side. Dr. King went a step further to prove the discrimination by moving into an apartment on the West Side in his fight against segregated housing. There were photos taken of King living in the small apartment and of him playing pool at a local establishment on the West Side.

The campaign eventually led to a race riot on the West Side of Chicago, which at the time was an all-white neighborhood, but nothing as hostile as the march at Marquette Park, in August of 1966. The hostility from the residents of the neighborhood was fueled by being subjected to racism. Dr. King was hit with a rock as bottles were thrown at the protestor. King later admitted he had never participated in a demonstration that was as violent and hostile as what he experienced in Marquette Park. Before the month ended, progress was made and the Chicago Housing Authority agreed to build public housing in predominantly white areas. In addition, Mortgage Bankers Association made mortgages available regardless of race or neighborhood. It was a remarkable campaign for blacks that lasted two years, and the Leaks were very much a part of the momentous events.

At that time, the Alfords made another addition to their family, welcoming their tenth child, Derrick Alford, who was born on August 3rd, 1966, becoming another bright light in the Alfords' life. They continued to rely on their faith to keep moving forward from a disaster that turned their world upside down. Glo was a religious woman, but she still struggled to comprehend why her beautiful babies had to die in such a horrific way.

Jimmy was still dealing with physical pain to the point that his body ached even from a simple task of raising his arms. Jimmy needed massages from the Alford clan just to loosen his tight muscles and soothe the constant pain. But he never complained or allowed his physical ailments to restrict him from his daily routines. Jimmy also silently carried the burden of wondering if he could have done more to save his children.

It wasn't long before the Alfords' home was back to being filled with company. Everyone still enjoyed gathering at the Alfords' house, enjoying Glo's wonderful cooking and being in the presence of such warmth.

The holidays, however, often brought on sadness among the Alfords. They tried not to get caught up in the sentiment of the holidays, but it was during those times the pain from their losses seemed greater. Nevertheless, it was Christmas the boys enjoyed most, as the Alfords splurged on presents to bring smiles to their faces. They didn't commemorate the birthdays of the children they lost, but it was obvious those days weighed heavy on their minds and hearts.

The Alfords didn't want Darryl and Derrick to suffer in any way from the silent grief they carried from the loss of their children. They still believed in a structured upbringing, and they wanted their two sons to be aware that life sometimes throws many curve balls, meaning that there are difficult times and bad things do happen, along with the good. Jimmy's number one priority was always to protect his family and to keep them safe. He raised Darryl and Derrick the same way he had his other children. He taught them early the difference between right and wrong so they could make wise decisions in their lives. Jimmy's strong principles continued to carry over into his profession, and he received more awards for outstanding achievement from the department in his role as a detective.

The painful memory of the children's death made Glo raise Darryl and Derrick being overprotective, as well as fearful. She didn't want them out of her sight for too long and often refused to allow them outside to play with their friends. Keith was older now and she had to give him more leeway, as he was growing into a man, but it didn't keep her from still worrying about him. Glo couldn't let go of the fear she lived with after losing seven children, and the family understood her apprehension. She was particularly paranoid about fire and stressed to the children to never play with matches or anything that could start a fire.

Darryl and Derrick engaged in normal sibling rivalry growing up, being so close in age, but yet so different in their ways. Darryl was more outgoing with a daring spirit, whereas Derrick was quiet and kept to himself. They looked at Keith as a second dad growing up and loved spending time with their big brother. The Alfords continued to provide a good life for their children, and it was an unspoken word not to mention the fire. In October of 1966, the Black Panther Party was founded by Bobby Seale and Huey Newton. It originated as a political organization, its main goal being to challenge police brutality in Oakland, California. The Black Panthers were responsible for many community social programs. It was an organization that had a huge impact on not only Oakland, but also New York City, Chicago, Los Angeles, Seattle, and Philadelphia. There were many who viewed the Black Panthers as criminals, whereas others saw them as one of the most influential black movement organizations of the late sixties.

On April 4th, 1968, the world was shocked by the assassination of Dr. Martin Luther King Jr., at age thirty-nine. Dr. King, along with a group of civil rights activists, was called to Memphis, Tennessee, to support a sanitation workers' strike. The night before King addressed a crowd at Mason Temple Church. The following day, while standing on the balcony outside his Lorraine Motel room, with a few other colleagues, including the Rev. Jesse Jackson, a sniper bullet struck Dr. King in the neck. He was pronounced dead at the hospital, leaving behind a wife and four children. There were many who believed Dr. King had a premonition of his own death, when he said, in his speech, "I've seen the promise land. I may not get there with you. But I want you to know, tonight, that we, as a people, will get to the promise land... I'm not worried about anything. I'm not fearing any man." Dr. King's death shattered many African Americans' hope for a promising future, and made them extremely angry. There were more than a hundred cities where people took their anger out by rioting, looting, and burning down buildings.

It took President Johnson, who was in office at the time, to plea with citizens to uphold Martin Luther King's commitment to nonviolence. However, Dr. King's untimely death caused the Fair Housing Act to be passed a week later. The campaign to outlaw discrimination in housing, which Dr. King had fought for two years, marked the last significant legislative achievement of the civil rights era. Dr. King will be forever remembered as the most prolific civil rights leader in our history and one of the greatest orators of all time.

Keith graduated from Simeon High School and decided to follow in his father's footsteps by joining the armed services. He joined the Marine Corps, where he could display the true meaning of dignity, respect, honor, and pride that his father instilled in him. In Keith's eyes, his father was and always would be his hero. He witnessed firsthand his father's daring attempt to rescue his siblings. Keith also witnessed his father's strength to keep going after such a devastating tragedy. He looked at any opportunity to show his appreciation for his father's exemplary example of manhood. That meant Keith developed the same attributes that kept his father so grounded and focused. He also learned to cope with the painful memories of that fatal night by burying it deeply in his soul, just like his father.

Keith left for a new adventure in life with the hope of making his parents proud. He successfully completed his course of study in Mechanical Fundamentals from the Department of the Navy. In addition, Keith satisfactorily completed a basic helicopter course at the Naval Air Technical Training Center. He also completed courses in H-46 Airframes and Utilities Organizational Maintenance and H-46 Power Plants and Related Systems Organizational Maintenance.

Keith's training prepared him for his assignment as a gunner assigned to the rescue team. He flew on one of the helicopters and sprayed the defoliant chemical, Agent Orange, during the war in Vietnam. It had damaging environmental effects in Vietnam, and many suffered long-term health issues. Keith was among the individuals exposed to the damaging chemical. After battling extreme medical issues, Keith was honorably discharged from the Marine Corps. He then returned to Chicago, where he continued to have severe seizures, as he attempted to move past the painful memories he had of Vietnam.

A FAMILIAR BOND

More than 50,000 soldiers who fought in the war in Vietnam didn't make it back home to their loved ones. Out of that alarming number of fatalities was Keith's best friend, Otis Andrews. Their friendship went back to early childhood and that close bond remained throughout the years. Keith would miss him immensely, but he was familiar with the pain of losing people dear to him. He was also aware of not allowing the bad punches life throws to defeat you. The tragedy of the fire made Keith grow up fast and more determined to succeed in life. He wasn't going to allow any setbacks to keep him from reaching his fullest potential. He never fully comprehended why he was chosen to be the one who escaped death, and that brought on much sorrow that remained locked inside of him.

The Alfords were elated to have their son back from the dangerous casualties of war. They continued to keep a close watch on their growing boys. Jimmy wasn't as overprotective as Glo, although he maintained a structured lifestyle, raising his sons. He had many layers to his personality and believed you have to play the hand that's dealt to you. He wanted to give his sons a fair chance in such a biased world. To Jimmy, that simply meant he implemented discipline and hard work and tried to remain focused through difficult and trying times.

Keith wasted no time getting settled back in Chicago. He immediately resumed his duties as big brother to Darryl and Derrick. He allowed them to tag along with him sometimes when he went out, something they enjoyed. Keith eventually married and had a daughter named Denise. He studied correctional training in college and became a guard at Statesville Prison. Keith's desire to go into law enforcement was another way to honor the man he respected so much. Keith entered the workforce with a mindset geared to capitalize on opportunities for advancement. He watched his father diligently over the years capture accolades that gave him self-satisfaction and financial compensation. Keith wanted to follow the same path and took his position as guard quite seriously. He was committed to his work from day one and that soon brought on recognition.

Keith developed the same outgoing personality that his father had and that took him even further. It was a perfect time to look for avenues to climb up the ladder of success. It was the beginning of the seventies, which marked a new era for African Americans. People of color were rising in areas such as politics, education, and business. It was during that time that the Congressional Black Caucus was formed. The caucus is made up of most African American members of the United States Congress. Their primary focus was to ensure that blacks benefitted from their constitutional rights. One of the founding members of the caucus, Shirley Chisholm, became the first black women elected to the United States Congress. She was also the first woman to run for the Democratic Party's presidential nomination. At that time, African Americans also began setting records in sports and entertainment. It was an optimistic time for African Americans, and Keith was among many who were eager to advance. Although Keith was dedicated to his position at work as a security guard, unfortunately his hard work and financial compensation weren't enough to keep his marriage going. He and his wife divorced, but he remained committed to his role as a father.

A routine visit to the courthouse for Keith turned into a twist of fate. When he spotted MaDear and her daughter, Mary, there for a traffic hearing, he was ecstatic so see familiar faces from a past that represented a good time in his life. It was a breath of fresh air to stand before people who knew the loving bond he shared with his brothers and sisters, instead of being reminded of the painful memory embedded in his soul and mind. After a warm embrace, Keith immediately inquired about JoAnn and made them promise to give her his well wishes. There had never been a connection between the two as kids, besides playing as children do. Therefore, it was nothing but the work of God that allowed Keith and JoAnn to reacquaint from that fateful day. They rekindled their familiarity as growing children and that foundation turned into a friendship. Their relationship eventually led to matrimony and the two families were elated over the connection.

Lovejoy was so happy that she accompanied Keith and JoAnn on their honeymoon. They traveled to Birmingham, Alabama, because Keith wanted to spend time with his father's side of the family. They stayed with his cousin, Al, who was the brother of Louis, the one who started the fire. Al was a prominent businessman in Alabama and the family didn't blame him for the careless actions of his brother. They had a wonderful time and were treated like royalty upon their arrival up until they departed. Keith and JoAnn had so much fun that Lovejoy's presence during their honeymoon didn't diminish it in the least.

They quickly adjusted to married life and acquired residence at 128th and Union. They had their own set of friends, but they also enjoyed each other's company. They had a lot of similarities and were both outgoing individuals. It was a perfect balance that allowed them to enjoy a fun and fulfilled life. They loved to go out dancing and Keith was very light on his feet. His over six-foot frame and heavy build didn't keep him from rhythmically gliding across the dance floor. Keith and JoAnn also loved to entertain. One of Keith's good friends, Mickey McGill, member of the R&B group The Dells, lived across the street. He and his wife would come over and play cards into the wee hours of the morning. It also was inviting to be at their home, because Keith was an excellent cook. One of his specialties was a scrumptious upside-down pineapple cake. He also enjoyed being out in the backyard on the grill when the weather permitted. JoAnn didn't spend as much time in the kitchen as Keith, but her pinto and great northern beans became one of Keith's favorite meals. It was surprising to Glo when she learned that Keith was eating beans, as he despised them growing up as a child.

Keith catered to JoAnn's every need and made his role as a provider top priority. JoAnn was definitely spoiled by her husband to the point that Glo couldn't believe that Keith purchased a dishwasher. Glo was from the old school when it came to taking care of the household, but Keith didn't mind picking up those duties. He did the household chores and made certain that everything functioned properly in the house. Keith was very active and even purchased expensive bikes for them to enjoy bike riding. JoAnn tried to accompany Keith by riding the bike to her mother's house, which was a couple of miles away, to get a feel for bike riding. But it wasn't to her enjoyment, so she parked the bike and decided that wasn't a sport she wanted to engage in. She was, however, supportive in helping Keith prepare for the bike marathons he participated in. Keith took pleasure in showering his wife with gifts and performing thoughtful gestures as a token of his love. He knew JoAnn loved banana splits and therefore he had one waiting for her in the freezer, since he arrived home from work fifteen minutes earlier than she.

It was acts of that nature that made Keith such a fun and loving guy. They even shared a common interest in pets, but JoAnn had a problem adjusting to Keith's dog. JoAnn owned twelve finch birds that she allowed to freely fly around the house. She didn't realize that people were fearful of them until she began to notice their reactions. They would duck and dodge to escape the path of the birds and often jumped out of their skins when the birds suddenly appeared. JoAnn decided it was best to keep the birds locked away while entertaining visitors.

However, nothing was more terrifying than the fear JoAnn had of Keith's dog, Keno. Keith had acquired the dog long before he and JoAnn got together, so he looked at his pet as part of his family. The dog was Doberman mixed with German shepherd and tall. Each time Keith walked through the door, Keno ran and placed his paws on Keith's shoulders. JoAnn tried to get used to the dog, but she was too afraid of him. Keith kept Keno in the basement and even purchased a child's gate to keep him from coming upstairs. Keno would come to the gate and watch JoAnn stir around the kitchen, but he never tried to go any further. JoAnn believed the gate ensured her safety, until one day she learned otherwise. Keith had a black velvet waterbed made with a heart shape in the middle and diamonds on the side, when waterbeds first came on the market. JoAnn and Keith were playing on the bed when Keno came charging in the room straight to JoAnn. She was terrified and just knew the dog was about to attack her. She screamed at the top of her lungs and Keith tried to calm her down. He tried to convince JoAnn that Keno was just looking to play, but she wasn't buying it.

JoAnn was adamant that she couldn't be under the same roof as Keno and be scared in her own house. Therefore, Keith was forced to move his dog dwellings outside in the garage. Then there was the time Keith had emergency surgery and had to be hospitalized for a few days. It was JoAnn who was left in charge of checking on Keno. She immediately called Jimmy over and made him tie the dog to a post in the yard. That allowed JoAnn to push Keno his food and water without feeling at risk of being harmed. By the third day of Keith being away was when Keno got loose. JoAnn was in the car leaving for work and noticed Keno running along the side of the car. JoAnn was startled by the dog's presence and had no idea what to do. Then she came up with the idea to call animal control. JoAnn informed her supervisor that she would be late for work and waited for them to show up. When they arrived, JoAnn gave animal control the dog's name. They called him, but Keno refused to go to the men. Finally, JoAnn was called over to the truck and told to call Keno's name. JoAnn pleaded for them not to allow the dog to harm her and explained that Keno belonged to her husband. JoAnn called for the dog and Keno came happily over to her. The men were then able to capture the dog, place him in the cage, and head to the pound. JoAnn felt terrible, but she was more fearful of Keno's presence than she was sad about his departure.

Keith came home from the hospital and got settled in to recuperate. It finally dawned on him that he hadn't seen or heard his dog. He asked JoAnn about Keno and she was forced to tell him that his dog was at the pound. Keith almost suffered a relapse when he sprung out of the bed in shock over the thought of his dog being gone. JoAnn attempted to calm him down, but Keith saw red. He couldn't fathom thinking that a dog that he raised since a puppy was at the pound. Keith was livid, but by the grace of God, one of his family members had picked Keno up from the pound. It was crazy times of that sort that brought joy and laughter into their marriage.

Keith's dedication to law enforcement showed his commitment to following in his father's footsteps. He was just like his father when it came to his job. Keith was serious and focused in his work. He wanted to be the big man on his job, like his father was down at the precinct. Therefore, he set a goal of becoming a warden at Statesville Penitentiary and began preparing to achieve that end.

Keith's tenacity with the job often spilled over after work hours. One particular afternoon on Keith's day off, he and JoAnn were having lunch at Pepe's Taco in Roseland, when all of a sudden, a special bulletin flashed across the screen that a riot had broken out at the prison. Keith bolted to his feet and told JoAnn they had to leave. He sped home, dropped her off, and headed to the jail. Even though it wasn't his scheduled day to work, Keith's dedication to his position by far exceeded his regular scheduled shift.

Her husband's dedication to his job prompted JoAnn to want to see if the place Keith talked about so much was what she pictured, so Keith brought her to Statesville Penitentiary for a tour. It happened to be during the time Richard Speck was a prisoner there. He was a mass murderer, who tortured, raped, and murdered eight student nurses at South Chicago Community Hospital. Speck was originally sentenced to death, but the sentence was later overturned to a life sentence. JoAnn got an opportunity to peek into Speck's jail cell and get a glimpse of the man responsible for such heinous crimes. It was definitely an experience for her to get an up-close look at the profession her husband took so much satisfaction in.

Keith and JoAnn were definitely making great memories together. They enjoyed sharing themselves with others and making people happy. A great example of that was the surprise party they hosted for their mothers. Keith and JoAnn had a special love for their respective mother-in-laws because they had raised them. So they decided to tell Glo and MaDear that the party was for the other one. Their birthdays were less than a week apart, and it turned out to be a perfect plan. The party was simply a beautiful event and both sides of the family were present. Glo and MaDear were pleasantly surprised at the thoughtfulness of their children. The food was scrumptious and plentiful. There was enough to accommodate the huge crowd, thanks to Lovejoy and JoAnn. It was a wonderful day filled with love and happiness, and it made Keith and JoAnn feel good to make their mothers happy.

For all the wonderful times that Keith and JoAnn shared, there was still a void inside of Keith that could never be filled. The tragic loss of his siblings was like a dark cloud hovering over his head. That painful memory of being the sole survivor of such a traumatic event never left him. It was even difficult for Keith to be in the old neighborhood, because the vision of that dreadful night would come rushing back like a terrible nightmare.

There was one occasion when Keith and JoAnn were visiting her uncle on the West Side, which was a block away from where the fire took place. JoAnn looked around and noticed that Keith had disappeared. She had a strong feeling of where he had escaped to. She walked down the street and found Keith standing in front of his old home, broke down in tears. It didn't matter how much time had passed, the pain was still so fresh as if it happened yesterday. JoAnn knew the hurt that Keith carried from that ordeal was something she could never heal.

She did everything in her power to be supportive when those depressing times arose. JoAnn visited the cemetery with Keith whenever he gained the strength to go. Keith also still battled severe seizures from the effects of the war in Vietnam. Although he received treatment and took medication for the seizures, it was a medical condition that he would have to contend with for the rest of his life, just like the pain of losing his siblings. Keith was still very committed to being in his daughter's life. Therefore, Denise spent a lot of time at the house with him and JoAnn. Keith was a very attentive and loving father, which was another quality JoAnn adored in her husband.

They would wake up early Saturday morning and go to the Pancake House on 95th Street. Keith loved waffles and the friendly atmosphere in the restaurant. Keith and JoAnn always sat at the table and observed all the families there having breakfast. They discussed having children of their own and even pictured their child sitting in a high chair at the table with them. That vision soon became a reality as Keith and JoAnn prepared to welcome a child into the Alford family.

WHY ALWAYS US?

Keith and JoAnn had a beautiful baby girl on August 31st, 1976. It was a welcoming addition to the Alford family and the parents couldn't be happier. This was JoAnn's first child and she poured all the love a mother could give into her daughter. She had a shining example of a mother's undying sacrifice to her children from watching MaDear and Glo over the years. They were both a part of her transition from a young girl to now, motherhood.

Keith and JoAnn wasted no time pampering their new bundle of joy. Felicia was quickly introduced to the finer things in life to the extent that her parents spoiled her. She even had a live-in nanny to help her parents. JoAnn understood more than ever the incredible loss Glo endured losing seven children. She bonded immediately with Felicia and already couldn't imagine life without her.

Glo spoke about the tragedy of losing her children to the people she loved and who were close to her. JoAnn was one of those people who Glo felt comfortable talking to about an incident that changed her life forever. It was always on her mind because Glo missed her children profusely. Although Glo had Keith and two more sons, she was tormented with what could have been and what should have been had that tragic night not occurred. Glo didn't carry the physical scars that covered Jimmy's body, but the emotional scars were just as painful. She and Jimmy tried visiting the cemetery, but the trauma for him was too much to handle.

Jimmy internalized a lot, so he continued to focus on being the strong father, a protector, and a provider for his family. In order to accomplish that, Jimmy couldn't express how much losing his children hurt him. It was then decided in the best interest of Jimmy's health that the Alfords wouldn't visit the children's gravesite. The Alfords were definitely hands-on grandparents for both of their granddaughters. Denise lived with them for a few years, while her mother pursued a career. The Alfords made sure they nourished them with love and support and gave them a stable upbringing.

Jimmy continued to pour his energy into his work and was proud that Keith was following in his footsteps with his dedication to law enforcement. By this time, Jimmy was a sergeant at the Wentworth District Police Department. Keith now had two daughters to take care of, and watching Jimmy's career accelerate made him become even more committed to climbing the ladder of success. He was now a captain with the Illinois Department of Corrections and was also teaching classes at the Correctional Training Academy. Keith's focus was dead set on becoming the warden for Statesville Penitentiary. He was willing to do whatever it took to achieve that goal. He loved the challenge of working extra hours and studying for the courses he was enrolled in. The training he received would prepare him for the position he was seeking. Once Keith landed that position, he would go to Springfield. The staff from the John Harvard Association felt Keith was the only candidate that knew what a correctional system should consists of. Keith received letters from Governor Dan Walker and Governor James R. Thompson for his great contributions to the state of Illinois. There was no denying his strong work ethics and his commitment to implement change behind the prison walls.

African Americans continued to thrive in the upcoming years. In 1977, Andrew Young became the first African American to become a U.S. Ambassador to the United Nations. It was also the year that the mini-series *Roots* aired on national television. It was the first program to depict the impact that slavery had on America. The series achieved the highest ratings for a television program. By 1978, Minister Louis Farrakhan revived the Nation of Islam, providing blacks another avenue to express their heritage and beliefs. Also in 1978, O'Grady became Superintendent of the Chicago Police

Department. His area of expertise where he gained recognition was police corruption, and he promoted the first black woman to the rank of Sergeant.

It was February of 1979, a month the Alfords saw as a dark time in their lives. They couldn't help but reflect on a month that wiped their family and dreams totally away. Although they tried desperately to hide their grief during that time, it was evident that February was a time of year that brought on sadness and depression. The night of February 8th, 1979, was a typical evening. Keith made it home from work and ate a delicious meal prepared by Glo before he resided to his downstairs bedroom at the Alford home. He got settled and began to unwind from a long day at the job.

Sometime in the early morning hours of February 9th, 1979, Keith prepared for bed, and as he hung his robe on the corner of the door, a seizure came on him before he could lie down. His full weight hit the bed so hard that it caused the bed to break, but no one heard him in distress, because by now everyone was asleep. The next morning, Glo prepared breakfast for the family. Everyone gathered at the table, and after some time passed, they realized that Keith hadn't come upstairs to join them. Jimmy went downstairs to investigate and found Keith lying in the bed facedown. Jimmy gingerly walked to his bedside and touched his body. It was very cold and his feet were white. There was acid on his lips and rigor mortis had set all the way down to his feet.

Jimmy stood there with an expression of stunned surprise, and although he knew his son was dead, it appeared surreal to him. In that moment, he kept wondering how he would break the news to his family. It was going to be extremely difficult to tell his wife that the son they were so proud of and who had survived that terrible fire was now dead at the tender age of twenty-eight. Jimmy knew he couldn't prolong the inevitable and braced himself to deliver the terrible news. He had been in this position of making heartbreaking announcements of this nature countless times as an officer. Jimmy gathered Glo, his mother, Lovejoy, and his two sons together. He took a deep breath and said, "I have to tell you all something. Keith is dead."

The family was completely shocked and grief-stricken. The devastating news almost took Glo out. She had dedicated so much love and energy into Keith after her other children passed away. He was her everything and her pillar of strength during the worst time in her life. To lose Keith in her home while she was upstairs asleep just about did her in. She reflected back to her last interaction with her son, which was Keith enjoying what would be his last meal prepared by his mother. Glo was heartbroken and wished it was her instead of Keith because she felt he had such a bright future ahead of him. Glo knew that she had to find the strength to deal with the unexpected death of her son for the sake of Darryl and Derrick. But she couldn't help but question why she and Jimmy had to always bury their children prematurely.

Darryl and Derrick ran downstairs to see Keith's body. Darryl was thirteen at the time and Derrick was twelve. They observed the brother they had looked upon as a second father lying there dead. Jimmy made sure that they didn't touch the body and demanded for them to go back upstairs. The boys were shocked to the point that they had a difficult time comprehending what had transpired. It was almost a blessing that Denise had moved back with her mother by the time of Keith's untimely death. It spared her the trauma of having to face such a devastating death at such a young tender age. The thought of Denise being in the household, while her father lay dead downstairs, would have been traumatizing for a five-year-old and too much to bear. The family contacted Leak Funeral Home to come and pick up Keith's body. The Leaks were taken aback to learn the Alfords had lost another child. They deeply sympathized with the family for having to go through another unexpected and heartbreaking loss.

It didn't take long before the Alfords' home was flooded with police officers and detectives. The detectives were overwhelmed that Jimmy had lost another child and they were there to extend their fullest support. Shortly afterwards, a grief-stricken JoAnn pulled up with two-year-old Felicia. There, sitting on the porch, were a distraught Darryl and Derrick. They were so glad to see JoAnn, because they had no idea how to comfort Glo. JoAnn carried Felicia into the house and gathered with the family to grieve the shocking loss.

Jimmy stood downstairs in the rumpus room by the bar talking to his colleagues. They admired and respected Jimmy for being able to be so philosophical and accepting. He was stoic and composed, until he laid eyes on Felicia, walking toward him with her little arms stretched out. Jimmy picked up his granddaughter and held her in his arms. He broke down in tears like a newborn baby, because Felicia, who was definitely Keith's twin, represented the son who had just departed this world. It was such a defining moment for a man who was programmed to shield himself from that type of emotion.

Keith Alford died from what is called a nocturnal seizure, a disorder he developed being assigned to helicopter rescue in the war in Vietnam. Keith was buried in Lincoln Cemetery next to his seven brothers and sisters. The Alfords only had the will to visit the gravesite a couple of times, since it had such a detrimental effect on Jimmy. The condolences to the Alford family came pouring in. Keith had made such a huge impact on so many lives during his short time on earth. His fellow employees at the Correctional Academy were deeply saddened by the news of his untimely death. His cheerful and outgoing personality would certainly be missed by all the lives he touched. It was yet another tragedy for the Alford family during the month of February. It was a good thing that Glo had Darryl and Derrick, because she could have easily withered away. Her remaining two sons and Jimmy gave her the will to keep on living. Jimmy believed that misfortunes can happen to anyone and one must learn to persevere. He felt that we never know what we can endure until we are put to the test. But the Alfords had to wonder, in the back of their minds, why always us?

The Alfords immediately became hands-on grandparents to both Denise and Felicia. Jimmy stepped up, not only as a grandfather, but also as a father. He didn't want his granddaughters to miss out on anything that they would have shared with Keith. Jimmy knew the importance of having a male role model in a child's life. The mere fact that Denise and Felicia no longer had their father around was enough incentive for him to shower the girls with all the love and support he could give them.

He spoiled Felicia Shawnta', being the baby of the family, and affection-ately gave her the nickname, Shawnie, from the song, "Shawnee River." It was a song that was known as the official state song of Florida, and tourists would come from all over to see the river in Florida that the song was written about. When Jimmy looked into his granddaughter's eyes, he saw a face of innocence, oblivious to the trials and tribulations of the world. He wanted to protect and shield her from all the difficult twists and turns one often encounters in life. Nothing gave the Alfords more gratification than making Shawnie happy, as she was a constant reminder of the son they adored and lost all too soon. The high expectations that were attached to being an Alford were easily passed on to her.

BORN INTO TRAGEDY

I recall my childhood filled with fond memories of being around my grandparents. I was spoiled rotten and definitely my grandfather's princess growing
up. Grandma nurtured me with an abundance of love and was extremely
overprotective. She didn't want her children or grandchildren out of her
sight for too long. Grandma would often times worry and pace the floor
until we were back in her presence. I didn't understand her apprehension
until I became wiser. My sister and I were the children of the only surviving
child of the fire. To lose my father after he escaped the walls of death was
a lot for my grandparents to contend with. It was as though under no
circumstances could they lose me or Denise. Although Granddaddy was
lenient, he wanted us protected at all cost, to the point that he insisted that
Darryl and Derrick allow me to tag along with them almost everywhere
they went.

I was now the only grandchild around most of the time, since Denise
and her mother had relocated to another city. My grandfather meant the
world to me, especially because he stepped up as a father in my life. He
made a meaningful impact in the very beginning to pave the way for me
to have a good life. As I grew older, I learned my grandfather was a man of
strength and courage and principle who carried everything on his shoulders
no matter how difficult the load became. And he expected the same from his

heirs. We dared not wear the face of shame and disappointment no matter what difficulties came our way. His military background and position on the police force were definitely present in the household. He taught us to spread our shoulders, stand tall, lift our chins, and hold our heads up high, regardless of the situation. That was instilled in me at an early age and remains with me to this day. I was the apple of my grandfather's eyes, and he wanted me to succeed in life. I was also blessed to have the presence of my uncles, from both sides of the family, to keep me safe and secure.

I was extremely close to Darryl, but my relationship with Derrick was quite the opposite growing up. He was the baby of the children born to the Alford clan and was quite spoiled. But he didn't get the same attention and the catering to that I received from my grandparents. It caused us to develop a slight rivalry because he felt I was a spoiled brat. Derrick received many tongue lashings from me reporting back to my grandparents all his mischievous behavior. I found it quite humorous when he was reprimanded for his unbecoming conduct. Derrick even used to tease me by saying I was discovered in a garbage can, so the family decided to adopt me. Our feud was simply a harmless battle for attention because we truly loved each other as family. Derrick wouldn't allow any harm to ever come my way, despite our constant bickering.

The relationships with the men in my family helped fill a void in my life of not having a father. I was much too young at the time of his untimely death to be able to cherish any memories of his presence. I learned from my grandparents, other family members, and from seeing photos that I was a spitting image of him. My body type, mannerisms, and the choice of words that came out of my mouth were a carbon copy of my father's.

As a young girl, I began to overhear family members whispering bits and pieces of information revolving around an incident that shattered the Alford household. In time, I came to learn of the tragedy in February of 1964 that claimed the lives of my aunts and uncles. The concealed pain that burned like the fire that snatched my grandparents' children away turned into a silent numbness inside of me. There were questions in my mind about that horrible day that were considered forbidden territory. There were light bulbs that shined from the darkness surrounding the story, and despite my curiosity, the missing pieces of that bizarre incident still remained an enigma to me. No one in the family wanted to trigger any sadness in two people who now lived a life of joy and peace as much as possible. The enormous respect we had for my grandparents restricted anyone from rehashing the suffering they endured for so long. Death had ripped a part of their souls that was buried along with their children in the cemetery.

It was their strength that taught me that life goes on and that you must continue to move forward with it. I felt connected to a tragedy that I had no concrete knowledge of, and the facts of that catastrophe that could only be confirmed by my grandparents remained a mystery to me. I witnessed with my own eyes depression seep into my grandparents' home. I often found granddaddy sitting in silence in heavy thought. Then there were times he used alcohol as a coping mechanism to numb the pain. My grandfather had emotional and physical pain that he carried throughout his life. I now understood the meaning behind the scars that covered his body. I was right there whenever he needed a massage to soothe his aches and pain. Throughout the years, despite it all, my grandparents remained focused on making me happy.

I remember one day asking Grandma if we could visit the cemetery as I was curious to learn more about the catastrophe. Grandma faced me with a stern look on her face and said, "No!" She had never responded to me so bluntly and seriously. We were paralyzed in silence until Granddaddy left for work. It was then that she felt compelled to explain the reason for her abruptness. Grandma told me that the few occasions they visited the cemetery were almost too much for granddaddy to handle, as it caused him to bleed from both his eyes and nose. For that reason, they vowed to never visit the cemetery again and I knew to never ask again.

However, I knew enough about the tragic fire to become curious with death. I was baffled by the fact that I felt as though my soul was connected to the tragedy. It was twice in my childhood, my father visited in my dreams to assure me that his spirit was still very much alive. The odds were against my father to escape the inferno, but somehow he did, and that resulted in my existence. It eventually opened my eyes to the realization that my purpose was greater than anything I could have imagined. I just didn't know exactly what it was.

The eighties represented a decade when African Americans continued to progress and prosper in many areas. There were still isolated incidents across the country where racism was evident, however. For example, in

1980, a riot broke out in Florida after police were acquitted of the murder of an unarmed African American man. The outcome was that fifteen people were killed in an incident that was compared to the deadly Detroit riot in 1967. In 1983, Chicago made history by electing the first African American Mayor. Harold Washington served in office until his untimely death in November of 1987. It was a time of unity in the city of Chicago, to get him elected, and together, we mourned his unexpected death. In the same year, President Ronald Regan signed a bill to declare Dr. Martin Luther King Jr.'s birthday a national holiday. By the end of the decade, African Americans were also being appointed to head coaching jobs in professional sports.

We continued to navigate through life with as much normality as possible. Derrick and Darryl decided to pursue careers in law enforcement. Darryl worked as a correctional officer and Derrick worked as a paralegal, wearing a suit and tie, for a few years, before also taking a job as a correctional officer. They took pride in following in their father and brother's footsteps. It was the beginning of the nineties, and I was now a teenager and quite mature for my age. I was responsible enough to have earned the privilege of receiving a brand new car, while only having obtained a driver's permit. However, Granddaddy had taught me how to drive at the age of twelve, long before I acquired my license.

I was around a lot of older people throughout my life, so I observed a lot that perhaps was too much for a young person to absorb. I was taught common sense and street smarts by my grandfather and uncles, but at the same time, I was still sheltered. My mother also had a strong impact on my life, as she is still an amazingly intelligent, independent, strong woman and a beautiful role model. I did, however, have a lot of freedom growing up, because my mother was a single parent, and during the earlier years, she was forced to work the swing shift.

I knew how to handle myself pretty well, but there were certain things that slipped through the cracks, and I went through a rebellious period. I was definitely a constant reminder of my father, because when people looked at me, they couldn't help but see Keith Alford. I remember one day going to visit my girlfriend at her grandparents' house who also live on Princeton. Her father kept staring at me until he finally said that that I looked like an old friend of his when he was younger named Keith.

I quickly asked him, "Was his name Keith Alford?" He confirmed that indeed it was. I smiled and said, "Keith was my dad."

His eyes filled with tears as he asked if he could just hug me. He went on to tell me what great friends he and my dad were before he passed. I loved hearing wonderful stories about my father and how great of a man he was. It gave me a strong desire to want to someday make my dad proud.

In May of 1993, Rev. A.R. Leak passed away. The city of Chicago mourned a community activist and the proud owner of two funeral homes. Leak had dedicated his time and service to assisting African Americans throughout his life. He played a huge role in bringing Dr. King to Chicago in the sixties during the civil rights movement. In addition to helping feed and clothe the homeless and poor, he also was instrumental in helping to establish more than a dozen Baptist churches around the city of Chicago. The Alfords were among the families touched by the generosity of the Leaks. They had a bond that was established almost thirty years ago. My grandparents felt the impact of his loss, but knew his powerful legacy would live on.

Mr. Spencer Leak Sr. had already stepped into his father's position as head of Leak Funeral Home. A catastrophe at a downtown nightclub resulted in a stampede that left twenty-one dead between the ages of twenty-one and forty-three. The Leaks provided funerals for at least nine of those families without adequate funds. It was just who they were!

By the end of the year, an incident occurred that would have a huge impact on my life.

My close-knit relationship continued with Darryl, despite him being married now with two sons. He had two boys, Darryl Jr. and Keith, the namesake of the brother he lost too soon. My grandparents now had two granddaughters and two grandsons to carry on the Alford name, which made them quite happy.

It was the week of the Thanksgiving holiday, and the time of year that I looked forward to enjoying my grandma and great-grandmother's delicious cooking. Darryl unexpectedly stopped by to visit with me that Friday, and we had a seemingly odd, but serious, discussion. It was a conversation like no other we had ever engaged in before. He was going through a difficult period in his life, brought on by the separation of him and his wife. I sat and took in every word and emotion he wanted to share. As he looked at me, I could see the pain deep within his eyes, and I was staring back at a broken man. Like most, my uncle wore a smile on the outside to others, but he couldn't fool me. I saw right through the happy face, because I could instantly feel his pain. I knew my uncle was depressed no matter what mask he was wearing.

As we conversed, I remember distinctly telling him no matter what was going on in his personal life, don't ever leave his sons. Denise and I were left without a father, and I didn't want his kids to experience the same sense of desolate. Honestly, I don't know from that day to this day what made me say that to him. Darryl left the house, promising to return on Monday, to take me to the gun range. Well, that day arrived, and instead of a visit, I received the dreadful news that Darryl was dead! I was devastated beyond consolation. I couldn't accept that the man who stepped in my life as a second father was gone at twenty-eight, the same age as my father when he departed this world, ultimately leaving two kids without their father, just as my dad left two kids behind. As the Alfords prepared to say goodbye to another loved one, the sympathy for the family once again poured in. It appeared our family was cursed by tragedy that was almost too much to bear. Everyone was deeply saddened that my grandparents had to endure this unimaginable pain yet again.

The Thanksgiving holiday was sad and gloomy. Instead of enjoying the day with laughter and festivities, my grandparents were preparing to bury their ninth child in the upcoming days. I knew the Thanksgiving holiday would never be the same for me. I reflected back to my and Darryl's last conversation, and in hindsight, it was as if he knew something I surely didn't. The morning of the funeral, I tried to gain the strength to say goodbye to a man who meant the world to me. I picked the suit for Darryl to be buried in and I opted to wear a matching colored dress.

I was so weak and fragile that I collapsed going up the stairs to the church. The services were held at Harvey Memorial Community Church on the South Side of Chicago. I watched my grandparents keep their composure throughout the funeral, once again having to display a tremendous amount of strength to get them through a difficult situation. When it was time for the family to view the body for the final time, I stood at the casket in disbelief. I felt numb and couldn't move until my mother came and led me back to my seat. I have never witnessed to this day a funeral procession as long as the one for Daryl Alford. His colleagues from the County Sheriff Department were all present along with so many friends and family, because he was such a great guy.

We pulled into Lincoln Cemetery for Darryl to be buried alongside his other siblings. It didn't seem fair or justifiable that so many of my family members occupied space at this cemetery so early in their lives. It was at the gravesite that grief overtook Grandma. The reality of having to bury yet another child was heartbreaking. Grandma's and my knees buckled at the same time, as Darryl was being lowered in the ground. It was Derrick who held me and others caught Grandma so we wouldn't hit the pavement. There were people standing at the entrance of the cemetery waiting for the family hearse to exit. They couldn't get in because it was so crowded, but they still wanted to show their support and wave as we drove by.

Darryl's death was a terrible tragedy. I stayed in bed for days following the funeral and drifted into a deep depression. I wouldn't eat or communicate with anyone. My emotional distance had my mother quite concerned, and she called the pastor to the house to pray over me. This was a dark period in my life, and I turned to alcohol just to numb the pain, as other family members had done. I walked around believing I was going to die by the age of twenty-eight as well. It didn't seem far-fetched since my dad and uncle had perished at that age. I was eventually forced to pick up the pieces and function in the real world. But it appeared quite evident that I was born into tragedy and to me it made my future quite uncertain.

WIND BENEATH
MY WINGS

As always, the Alfords were forced to show resilience after the unexpected passing of their ninth child and move forward. The Alfords' curse was sudden death and silencing your pain no matter how much was internalized. Time passed on and I eventually found a place of calm peace at the cemetery visiting loved ones. It became a safe haven for me, sitting quietly meditating.

I had one of my first realizations of the strength it takes to get back up after being knocked down from the death of Daryl. We weren't the type of family that would seek counseling. I would rather sit on a bench and talk with a total stranger than to lie on a therapist's couch. The strength taught to me by my grandfather became my key to survival. He was retired now, which gave me more time to spend with him.

During my grandfather's career, he had received many commendations for outstanding work performance up until his retirement date. Then it was time for my grandfather to enjoy a well-deserved break from the demands of a high-profile job. He could truly rest his aching body from the physical trauma he endured from the fire. Granddaddy had lived with one lung since the incident and it was starting to take a toll on him. The time came when Granddaddy began to succumb to his physical ailments. He had been diagnosed with chronic obstructive pulmonary disease. It finally came to a point that Granddaddy was placed in hospice care. Their job consisted of keeping him comfortable, because medically there was nothing else that could be done for him. They would give him morphine, as needed, to lessen his pain, as he made his transition.

I became extremely concerned and vented my frustration with the nurse. In my mind, I felt they were there to help kill him, instead of being of assistance. I was in denial and couldn't accept that it was time for my grandfather to depart this world. But I couldn't hide from the realization that the presence of hospice meant that he was going to die. I came to the house every day and witnessed my grandfather deteriorate right in front of my eyes. On one visit, my mother and I came and found him smoking a cigarette with the oxygen tank on.

My mother was frightened, as she began to back out the door, yelling, "Jimmy, now you know you're not supposed to be smoking with these machines on in here."

His reply was that he was going to die anyway.

My mother looked at me and said, "I'm getting out of here. Are you staying?"

"If the machines blow, then I guess I'm dying with him," I replied.

She shook her head and closed the door behind her. I stood at the foot of the bed and watched the man I admired, with every breath in his body, cling to life.

The following day when Mom and I arrived, Granddaddy wasn't as lucid. My mother asked if he had seen his kids, and he nodded his head yes with a smile on his face. I then asked if he saw my father, and a tear welled up in his eye.

The next morning, I got a call at home from Grandma informing me that I needed to get to the house. I frantically called my mother, as I gathered my belongings and rushed out the door. When I got in my car and realized the gas hand was on empty, all I could do was scream oh no. I arrived at the gas station and pleaded with God to let me get there in time. People were looking at me like I was crazy, but I didn't care. My only focus was to get to my grandfather before he took his final breath. However, there was something inside of me that made me feel I wasn't going to make it there in time. I sped through the streets and ran countless red lights, trying to get there as fast as I could. There were cars coming, but I just blew the horn, as I crossed the intersections and prayed I didn't get hit. I pulled up in front of the house, where Derrick was standing outside. I ran right past him and up the front steps.

I rushed through the door and found Grandma sitting on the couch. She looked at me and said, "He went five minutes ago."

I dashed up the stairs, straight to Granddaddy's bed, and rested my head on his chest. His body was still warm, as I climbed into bed. I had tears in my eyes, but I was okay, because I got an opportunity to lie with my granddaddy one final time.

Later, Leak Funeral Home arrived to pick up the body. I couldn't watch, so I went and joined my grandmother on the couch. When I saw them coming down the stairs with Granddaddy in the body bag, that's when it hit me. I started screaming because I had never witnessed this process of death, despite all the losses that we suffered. Images of members of the family who were deceased then came flashing through my mind. I felt totally lost, wondering what was going to happen now that my hero was gone.

This marked the day that I felt the pain of losing a dad. Although I carried the pain of not having a father, it wasn't as piercing, because I had my grandfather. Darryl's death had a huge impact on my life, and now Granddaddy had passed. I felt that all the men who had ever loved me unconditionally, as only a father could, were gone.

James Edward Alford Jr. departed this world on February 9th, 2000, and people celebrated his life on February 12th. At the funeral, his colleagues from the department that were lucky enough to cross paths with Granddaddy spoke of his strength and courage. My grandfather touched many lives throughout his journey. His remarkable faith and outgoing personality helped brighten the lives of everyone who came in contact with him. Granddaddy looked at life for what it was, which was a journey, even with the physical scars that remained permanently on his body. I felt extremely proud to see all the lives that my grandfather touched.

As I looked at my grandmother, I couldn't help but feel deep compassion and sorrow. This courageous woman had been strong through circumstances that could have snatched away her will to keep going. She now faced life without the man she had spent fifty years with. My grandfather was not just her husband; he was also her best friend, as they always had each other to lean on. Together, they were able to rise above hurdles that may have otherwise diminished their faith. I had nothing but admiration for two individuals whom I felt honored to have as grandparents. Granddaddy was transported to his final resting place at Lincoln Cemetery.

We traveled down a familiar path as we said our final goodbyes to our hero. As the tears flowed, I thanked God for the strength and endurance that my grandfather instilled in me.

When I encountered the joy of motherhood, fears and paranoia began to set in. I was overly protective because I didn't want to lose my children, especially to an unfortunate accident. Those feelings stemmed from having separation issues.

Over the years, I continued to fight a battle with being overly cautious. I have a tremendous fear of fire and exercise every measure to reduce the chances of such a tragedy occurring. I can be lying in bed asleep and wake up with an unsettled feeling. That causes me to wake up my children and make them get in bed with me. I've even gone as far as to walk up to their bedsides in the middle of the night and get close to their faces just to make sure they're still breathing. One day, I received a phone call from my grandmother requesting to see me. I always honored Grandma's wishes, so I made my way to her house that morning. We sat around the table, engaging in small talk, until she got up and walked to the china cabinet, where she took out a stack of pictures, newspapers articles, and other publications. She walked back and placed the items in front of me, softly saying, "I want you to have this."

As I glanced at the items, the photos of the children, displayed on top of their caskets, at the funeral, stood out. There were no further words exchanged because we both knew that we had embarked on a painful memory that had stayed buried for too long. I took the items home and tucked them safely away. I knew that Grandma had entrusted me with a part of the Alford legacy that couldn't be erased.

In June of 2004, another Alford earned her key to the pearly gates. My great-grandmother Martha Lovejoy, made her transition. She passed on when she was over a hundred years old. Her work here was truly complete, and among the many things that were said, was, " Job well done!" Mother Lovejoy joined the other Alfords that day at Lincoln Cemetery.

Years passed and my grandmother's health challenges soon took a toll on her body. It was a ritual for just Grandma and me to have pancakes and coffee most Sunday mornings. I always loved Grandma's pancakes as a kid, and nothing had changed. It was approaching our scheduled visit, and I realized I hadn't heard from her in a few days. I called Grandma, and she informed me that she wasn't feeling very well. I went straight to her house and found her lying on the couch. She didn't look very good and appeared rather lethargic. I pulled back the blanket she was wrapped in and discovered her feet were swollen and had turned shades of purple and blue. I yelled, call 911, and shouted, "She's had a heart attack!"

Derrick, a cousin, and I took Grandma to the hospital, and the doctors informed us that she had suffered multiple heart attacks. Grandma was hospitalized for about a month, and during that time, she lost a substantial amount of weight. She was finally released to come home under hospice care. Derrick did everything in his power to care for her, but two weeks later, she had to be taken back to the hospital. The doctors wanted to perform surgery on her, but Grandma refused. There wasn't anything Derrick or I could do to override her decision because she was still of sound mind to make her own medical decisions. The day that Grandma passed was the day that she was scheduled to be released from the hospital.

The night before, I rushed there from work and made it right in time before visiting hours ended. When I arrived at the hospital, she had been moved to a different floor. I walked into Grandma's room and was stunned when she said, "Hey Shawnie, what took you so long?"

I was nearly speechless to see her eyes so bright and that she had the strength to speak so clearly. I became excited, because it appeared that Grandma was recovering. I quickly reminded her that she was going home tomorrow, and Grandma softly said, "Yes, I'm going home."

She then asked for me to give her a drink of water. She took a sip from the straw, and I could literally hear the water traveling through her frail body. Grandma let out a big sigh, and I asked her if she was tired, and if she was ready to see her kids and Granddaddy.

She smiled and said, "Yes."

I held back the tears, as I grabbed her hand and told her it was okay if she was ready to see all her babies and husband. I then asked Grandma if she was worried about Derrick.

"Yes," she said.

I reassured her that he was going to be okay, and I was not going to leave him. I kissed her and told her I'd be back in the morning to bring her home, and left the hospital for the night.

The next morning, I received a phone call from Derrick informing me that I needed to come to the hospital, which I was going to do anyway. I rushed to get there and was in disbelief because she was just lying there and was no longer hooked up to any monitors. Searching for answers, I found the nurse. She explained to me that Grandma asked her for a cup of coffee, and when she returned with it, Grandmother had passed.

Once again, I climbed into her bed and lay close to her, crying and telling her, "I'm sorry. I didn't mean it." I regretted telling her it was okay to leave, and I felt in doing so that her passing was my fault. I beat myself up for ignoring the obvious signs the night before. After all, I had seen it many times over. The burst of energy she got, accompanied by bright, glossy eyes, sometimes happens not long before a person makes their transition. I call it the look of death.

When I made it home, I retired to my place of meditation, which was the bathroom. I sat down in complete darkness. At that moment, I had a vision in which Grandma appeared, wearing a white gown, a halo, and wings. She was letting me know that she made it home, and it was okay. I miss my grandparents profusely, but they will always be the wind beneath my wings!

Gloria Esther Alford departed this world on January 18th, 2007, to be with the Lord and the rest of the Alford family members that had passed on. Grandma's homecoming was held at Harvey Memorial Community Church and Leak & Sons Funeral Home handled the service. Grandma was remembered as a woman dedicated to her family who provided strength and courage to everyone she came in contact with. Through her personal tragedies, her faith in God never wavered. Grandma was transported to her final destination at Lincoln Cemetery. My grandmother will forever remain in the hearts of the many people touched by her strength, great cooking, and love!

A WISH FULFILLED

In 2008, African Americans witnessed a time in history that was the biggest milestone thus far in our culture when the first African American was voted the forty-fourth president of the United States. President Barack Obama was elected on November 4th, 2008, and was sworn into office on January 20th, 2009, on Dr. King's holiday. More than a million people attended the inauguration, setting a record attendance for any event held in Washington, D.C. Our ancestors fought hard to see a day in which a black man would be allowed to run the country. President Barack Obama was able to implement change at a time of economic despair in the United States. His presidency showed the world that there are no boundaries on the level of achievement for people of color. We lost a lot of great leaders in our fight for equality, but the journey produced our first black president. I knew my grandparents were smiling as President Barack Obama was sworn into office.

That milestone moment made me reflect on my grandparents' journey. My grandfather had always spoken of the ups and downs one encounters while traveling through life. Blacks suffered tremendously to gain their constitutional rights and finally were victorious. Dr. King had a dream, and it manifested when Barack Obama filled the highest seat in the country. It becomes the responsibility of future generations to keep the dream alive.

At that point, Denise still lived out of town. Derrick and his one son, my two children and I, Darryl's two children, and Keith's two children were the Alford legacy in a city where our roots were established. The responsibility was on Derrick and I to pass down what was instilled in us. We were both overprotective parents, and at the same time, we shared a lot of similarities when it came to our parenting. He also checked on his son periodically through the night to make sure he was still breathing. Derrick requires his son to check in with him every few hours if he's out of his sight. And of course there is the extra precaution to prevent a fire from occurring just like me. There were still unanswered questions lingering about the fire that made our worry and concerns legitimate.

Time passed and something began to nag at my spirit connected to the tragedy. Things began to occur in my life in which I felt Grandma's presence more than ever. She was always a spiritual woman and was blessed with the keen use of her third eye, the gate that leads to inner realms and spaces of higher consciousness. Grandma had an assignment she wanted me to carry out so that her soul could completely rest. I knew Grandma had given me the information regarding the fire for a reason. It was my responsibility to carry out her wishes that her children never be forgotten. Occasionally, over the years, I skimmed through the information, but when the emotion became too overwhelming, I would put it away. I struggled with embarking on a journey that would be painful, but the strength my grandparents had instilled in me would soon override my skepticism. They assured me in the spiritual realm they would be with me every step of the way!

Finally, I made a decision that I was going to tell the Alford story. I took the materials out and began to investigate everything left in my possession. I came across two binders in their original state and the ink was still legible. I began reading and realized it was a court deposition, an account from their own mouths of everything that occurred the day of the fire, my grandparents' sworn testimonies of the actual incident. I became overcome with emotion as I read through the documents. I had to take a break to gather my composure. It was surreal, reliving a time where I actually felt present, and it was confirmation that I was on the right track. My grandparents were about to guide me through a process that was going to change my life. I was hesitant to reopen a door that had been closed for decades, but I was more curious to finally get answers to questions that remained a mystery for so long.

I went through an array of emotions as I flipped through the pages. I sympathized with my grandfather when the questions became too much for him to bear. A few times during the deposition, my grandfather had to be allowed time to gather his composure. I visualized my grandmother as she described running to the neighbors for help. I could hear her voice as she screamed for someone to save her children. The tears ran down my cheeks as I read of the daring attempt by Granddaddy to rescue his children. My emotions quickly shifted as I learned more about the perpetrator responsible for the tragedy. I became angry when I thought about the carelessness of an individual who had cost my family members their lives. I couldn't believe all this information was right in front of my face and things were slowly being revealed.

The foundation was set for me to walk into a divine assignment. I closely examined photos of the children that were displayed on their caskets. Saddened by their premature departure at such an innocent age, I reflected on my own children and couldn't imagine life without them. Every media publication in the city of Chicago covered the story. The accounts of the incident in the newspapers coincided with the deposition but of course were not as detailed. There were pictures of the children featured throughout the papers with their names and ages.

This shocking tragedy even traveled to Birmingham, Alabama, the birthplace of my grandfather. By now, I was intrigued because I was discovering how a city came together during a time when racial tension was at its peak. My grandfather, being a highly respected detective, brought additional coverage to the story. I began to investigate further and located a reel that contained footage. I had no idea what it consisted of, but it was titled "Alford Children." I searched around until I found a place that could transfer it to modern technology. There were only a couple of minutes of footage, but every detail was pertinent information. It was the children's caskets being loaded in the cars at A.R. Leak & Sons Funeral Home.

A light bulb suddenly went off in my head, and I called my friend, Spencer Leak Jr., who has always considered the Alfords like family. I shared with Spencer a few details regarding the project I had taken on, and asked if he could set up an interview for me with his father. Mr. Spencer Leak Sr. was in charge of orchestrating the transporting of the children's bodies to the cemetery on the day of the funeral. I wanted to hear everything about that day and his relationship with my grandparents.

Nervously, I sat across from Mr. Spencer Leak Sr. and braced myself for this moment. There was silence as he reviewed the newspaper articles and flipped through the photos in deep thought. I could see by the expression on his face that he was reflecting back to a time that was still fresh in his memory. Next, I showed him the footage from the day of the Alford children's funeral. He was now ready to reveal what that period in time meant to the city of Chicago and how it involved my family.

He began by saying how much he admired the strength of my grand-mother and the courage of my grandfather. He was thinking back to the time my grandmother sat in front of him making plans to bury seven of her children. He then said, "I had never witnessed that kind of strength, considering the circumstances. Here in front of me was a woman who was small in stature and yet so brave, after losing seven of her children, and having a husband who was in the hospital, fighting for his life. "You should be proud. You come from good stock," he said, as he looked at me.

I shook my head in agreement because I felt honored to sit before him and represent my grandparents' legacy. Mr. Leak said it was a fantastic idea to tell this story, incorporating African American history into it. He gave me all the information he knew regarding the funeral service and burial. He was also able to share with me what was transpiring in the city of Chicago during that time. The Alford children's funeral was a big service for A. R. Leak & Sons Funeral Home, with countless to follow. He went on to tell me again how strong my grandmother was and how imperative it was to include that in the story. "Even the son who survived, she was a pillar of strength for him," he said. "We were looking at Keith, thinking that he's lost all his brothers and sisters. We were honored to have been able to assist in putting those beautiful babies to rest. Helping families in need has been our philosophy since opening our doors.

"We buried Flukie Stokes' son with a casket made to resemble a Cadillac Seville. He had walked in with all that drug money and paid for the funeral like it was nothing. But he had the right to a funeral like anyone else. After burying his son, the father was killed, and we buried him too. When you're in the funeral business, you can't choose who's going to come seeking your services. Mrs. Stokes cried as hard as any other person for her gangster son. We will continue to operate our business on lending a helping hand to those in need, and that extends past the funeral business," Mr. Leak said.

He gave me some pertinent information to include in my story, along with some of Chicago's African American history that I was unaware of. Before I left, Mr. Leak informed me that he would get in touch with a man named Jim O'Grady. He was above my grandfather at the police department, and Mr. Leak was certain he had some vital information that would be helpful. My adrenaline was flowing rapidly by now because things were definitely falling into place.

I called Mr. O'Grady and he agreed to meet me at a café near his home once he learned the nature of my call. Needless to say, I was a nervous wreck. My anxiety continued right up until I walked into the café and sat across from him. It turned out he was one of the nicest men I have ever met. Mr. O'Grady made me feel comfortable as soon as we made our introductions. My children accompanied me and sat in a booth behind us while I conducted the interview. Mr. O'Grady was enjoying retirement after a thirty-two-year career in the Chicago Police Department and then being elected Cook County Sheriff. Police officers have run for public office before in Chicago, yet few, if any, have galvanized the ranks as O'Grady did.

Mr. O'Grady looked straight into my eyes and said, "Your grandfather was a solid guy with integrity and honesty. He was a respectful and hardworking man." The high praise coming from Mr. O'Grady about my grandfather put a smile on my face. Mr. O'Grady went on to discuss my grandfather's strong work ethics. Next, we spoke in detail about the tragic fire and his involvement during that time.

O'Grady said, "We have had black officers and white officers killed throughout the years, and there's never been a difference how they're laid to rest at a wake or a funeral, because they were 'Blue.' Were there some terrible things going on in the country during that time? Definitely. Are things changing? Slowly. Hopefully, we'll get to the point where there's only a small minority of people acting like dopes. I remember the tragedy that befell James and his family. It makes me cry to this day just talking about it. It's the same feeling today that it was back then."

Mr. O'Grady took a moment and glanced at my children. He then smiled and said, "The good thing that came out of reliving this catastrophe is being able to meet James's family—the granddaughter who has the courage to tell the story, and how precious his great-grandchildren are! I know he'd be extremely proud!"

After several emotional pauses through our conversation, we shared a meal and ice cream with the kids. O'Grady embraced me and the kids before I thanked him for his time and we parted ways.

On the ride home, my daughter looked at me and said, "Mommy, I'm proud of you." That meant everything to hear those words come out of her mouth.

Next on the agenda was to sit down with my mother, JoAnn Alford, and uncle Derrick Alford. I knew I was opening up a can of worms that Derrick preferred to remain shut. But something in my heart was telling me talking about the incident would be therapeutic for the both of us. I arranged for my mother to come by one Saturday afternoon and we sat down at the dining room table to talk. The first thing I wanted to know from her was the mood on the day of the children's funeral. Her description was so heartbreaking that it brought tears to my eyes, as I visualized Grandma and my father enduring so much pain.

My mother then went on to discuss her relationship with the Alford family and how she got reacquainted with my father. I was hearing for the first time a personal side of my parents' relationship that my mother decided to share with me. It wasn't as if anything was kept a secret—there were just certain topics that we never discussed. My mother further confirmed what O'Grady and Leak explained about how the city of Chicago came together to assist a family in need, and how the outpouring of love and support for the Alford family was so overwhelming. She explained to me in detail the sadness and depression that my father lived with throughout his life. He never understood why his brothers and sisters had to die in that fire. He also expressed to my mother his confusion about why the cousin snatched the two younger children from his arms. It was difficult for Keith to live with those unexplained questions, which contributed to the physiological trauma he endured.

My mother shook her head and said, "I didn't understand what Keith was going through during our union together, mainly because we were still young and trying to figure out life. But now that I'm older I understand how unresolved issues can have a major impact on your life. The effects from that incident bothered Keith to the day he left this world."

As my mother reminisced, there were times in our discussion that brought on laughter. It was gratifying to have joyous occasions, instead of the dark cloud that often hovered over the Alford family. I was able to get an even bigger picture of this story after speaking to my mother. She provided me with insight that further explained a lot of unresolved issues. My mother is extremely proud of my decision to finally tell this story. After all, it was she who ultimately confirmed my thoughts of writing the story by relating Grandma's wishes that her children never be forgotten. It took months to gain the strength to dive into what was once considered forbidden territory. I no longer felt fearful, but instead determined to see this project completed.

I came to a point in the journey that proved be the most challenging. It was now time to sit down with Derrick. There was no one left in the Alford family that had been affected by our tragedies more than he. Derrick was the only surviving child out of the Alfords' ten children. He was reluctant to revisit such a traumatic event, but I believed together we could be each other's comfort through the process. The time had arrived to have a heart-to-heart talk with Derrick about the past and what writing this book meant to me.

We sat down and Derrick opened up the conversation by saying, "We never discussed the fire, and if it wasn't for my mother, I wouldn't know about it. The tragedy was something that always stuck with me, because I had other brothers and sisters, but never met them. Yeah, I think about it and wonder if my life would be different if they were still alive. I think about what kind of impact they would have had on my life. I'm proud of the life that I had as a child and of the parents who raised me. I respected my father's actions and the things he accomplished on the job. For the most part, it made me a better person. I never wanted to go into law enforcement; I guess it was something that just fell into my lap from the ties my family had with the law. I don't regret going into law enforcement because it shaped me as a man and the way I raise my son."

Derrick and I took a moment to exchange stories about how overprotective we are as parents. We both needed to hear that it wasn't unreasonable for us to have fears. The conversation became emotional when we spoke about the actual circumstances we knew about the fire and the physical toll it took on Granddaddy. Derrick had to excuse himself over the thought of his father having to miss his own children's funeral. Next, we talked about the impact that Keith's death had on him as a twelve-year-old boy. Losing my father unexpectedly was a damper in Derrick's life, since he looked at Keith as a second father. He got an opportunity to express his fear of not living past the age of twenty-eight, something I too struggled with, until that time passed. I never knew until that day that Derrick suffered with that same fear.

We had to stop the interview a few times to regroup. There were moments he had to wrap his arms around me and provide comfort. And certain issues were discussed in which I had to do the same for him. Through the tears, we were able to arrive at a point where Derrick discussed losing his father,

"When my father became sick, we all knew that he was going to die," he began. "Most of the time spent with him at the house was doing everything imaginable to make him comfortable. The one thing that stands out to me, now that we're talking about it, is I told my dad that I loved him tremendously. Knowing that his days were numbered, I reflected on all the things he taught me. I was present when my dad took his last breath. Although it was difficult, I can honestly say I was glad to hold his hand as he made his transition."

The room fell silent as Derrick and I reflected back to that day. We began to talk about Grandma and how we're able to relate to her over-protectiveness. Derrick then drifted into deep thought about his mother. Finally, he said, "I remember when my mother got sick and I was doing my best to take care of her. I was at home with one of my friends when she suffered another heart attack. The doctors wanted to perform surgery on her that she was totally against. I tried to convince her, but she was adamant about not wanting to go through it. I finally had no choice but to give in and honor her wishes. To this day, I wish I could have overridden her decision, but it was totally out of my hands."

Once again, Derrick and I found ourselves overwhelmed by the memories. We accomplished a major milestone by releasing the silence attached to the fire. It allowed us to lighten a heavy burden that weighted heavy on our hearts. We were now healing from an incident that has deeply affected us our entire lives. For me, it brings to the surface a pain that has been buried throughout the years. We live the aftermath of it day in and day out. I was able to face the reality that the tragedy surrounding my family has a lot to do with who I am today. My faith, hopes, fears, and how I cope with situations in my life, whether good or bad, are stemmed indirectly from that incident. It taught me how to survive. I had no prior knowledge of how this story would provide a source of strength for me. I was able to discover there were good people who helped my family even during a time when racism and segregation was at its peak. It was refreshing to learn that a bad situation could occur with a family where race didn't matter. It spoke volumes that people could put aside their prejudices to aid a family in distress.

This project brought on a sense of purpose in understanding what the Alford name truly represents. We can now have a true understanding of what it means to operate with perseverance, strength, and courage. I feel an abundance of weight has been lifted off my family and generations to come. My hope is that everyone who is touched by this story will realize the importance of family, strength, and courage. I also hope African American people are able to bring back the togetherness and unity that once made us an unstoppable force. We made historic leaps throughout this story, although there is still work to be done.

I had no idea that a year ago when I scheduled a date to finish this project I was picking the actual day of Thanksgiving, a holiday I have disliked since the passing of my Uncle Darryl. But maybe my angels above were showing me that it was time to release that burden as well, because now I had something that made me happy on a day that once brought complete sadness. The healing process is well underway, and I thank everyone involved for walking this journey with me!

Heroic Father Gets Award

HEROIC EFFORT to save his seven children from fire ended in tragedy, but Detective James Alford of Chicago Police department Area 4 robbery division is rewarded for his attempt. Alford [center] is presented with memorial fund check for $6,040.93 by Sal Russo [right], vice president of Cosmopolitan National bank of Chicago, and LeRoy Winbush, consultant to bank. Alford received broken leg and severe burns in futile rescue try.

Heroic Father

Gloria and Keith

Second Set Of Children Darryl and Derrick Alford

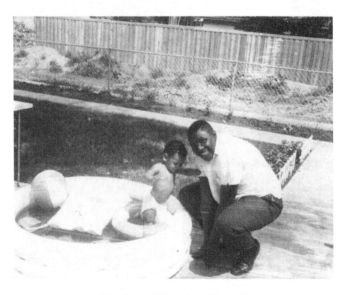

Keith and Brother Darryl

Keith In U.S. Marines 1968

Department of the Navy
Bureau of Naval Personnel

Service — Schools

This certifies that

KEITH W. ALFORD 2471980
PRIVATE, U. S. MARINE CORPS

has satisfactorily completed the prescribed course of study at the
Naval Air Technical Training Center, Millington, Tennessee
Aviation Machinist's Mate R(Reciprocating)Course, Class A

this 20th *day of* FEBRUARY , 19 69

G.E.Burke
U.S. NAVY, COMMANDING

NAVPERS 674 (REV. 4-63)
S/N 0105-401-3402

Department of the Navy
Bureau of Naval Personnel

Service — Schools

This certifies that

KEITH W. ALFORD 2471980
PRIVATE FIRST CLASS, U. S. MARINE CORPS

has satisfactorily completed the prescribed course of study at the
NAVAL AIR TECHNICAL TRAINING CENTER, MILLINGTON, TENNESSEE
BASIC HELICOPTER COURSE, CLASS C

this 10th *day of* APRIL , 19 69

C. L. Burbage
U.S. NAVY, COMMANDING

NAVPERS 674 (REV. 4-63)

Keith Alford's Achievments

Keith Alford Serving In Vietnam

CHICAGO POLICE DEPARTMENT

Honorable Mention

PRESENTED TO . . . .

SERGEANT JAMES ALFORD #975

2ND DISTRICT

FOR . . . .

On 7 Feb 1978 at 2335 Hrs a female negro, 26 years of age was found shot to death in her apartment at 5322 So. State St.

On 8 Feb 1978 Sgt. Alford, Officers Stephenson and Smith located a witness to the homicide who knew the offenders by nicknames. The officers conducted an extensive investigation and learned the true names of the wanted subjects. A stakeout of Projects in the Taylor Homes was set up after approximately four hours. The two subjects were later arrested. After further questioning by the officers one of the arrestees confessed that he had robbed and shot the victim. The officers continued to work around the clock and recovered the weapon used in the offense. One arrestee was charged with Murder, Felony Murder and Armed Robbery.

THIS FINE CALIBER OF POLICE WORK IS A CREDIT TO THE OFFICERS AND THE CHICAGO POLICE DEPARTMENT. THE DEPARTMENT SALUTES YOU AND HEREBY AWARDS THIS HONORABLE MENTION.

CONGRATULATIONS!!!!

Erskine Moore

RICHARD J. DALEY, *Mayor*

JAMES M. ROCHFORD, *Superintendent*

District Commander, 2nd District

DATE
21 July 1978

AWARD

Sergeant James Alford Honorable Mention Award

Capt Keith Alford 1978

Capt Keith Alford Instructing Day of Death

Keith Alford's grieving parents, James and Gloria, view an album with newspaper clippings on their loss of seven other children in a 1964 fire.

They lose 8th child: 'Why always us?'

Losing Keith

Mr. and Mrs. Alford Day of Keith's Death

They lose 8th child: 'Why always us?'

By Robert Enstad

THERE WAS no response Friday morning when the alarm clock went off next to the bed of Keith Alford, who lost seven brothers and sisters in a home fire 15 years ago.

Sensing something was wrong, Keith's father, police Sgt. James Alford, went downstairs to Keith's room to investigate.

"He was lying there face down, his body was very cold, and his feet were white," Alford said. "There was acid on his lips, and the rigormortis had set in all the way down to his feet."

ALFORD STOOD there for a moment, wondering what he would say to his family. It would be hard to tell them that the one child who had survived that terrible fire long ago, the son he and his wife, Gloria, were so proud of, was now dead — at the age of 28.

"Yes, we were mighty proud of Keith; he was going to get this big promotion and go to Springfield," said Alford, 51. "People from the John Howard Association said Keith was the only person who knew what a correctional system should be all about. He had letters from [former Gov. Dan] Walker, from [Gov.] Thompson."

By the time Alford returned upstairs, he said, he was thinking about how many times he had been in this role before as a Chicago policeman for 25 years and how he had handled it.

"My job calls upon me to make these announcements," he said. "So I gather together my wife, my mother, and the two sons I have left. I said: 'I have to tell you something. Keith is dead.'"

KEITH ALFORD, captain with the Illinois Department of Corrections, taught a class for correctional officers at St. Xavier College on West 103d Street.

On Feb. 21, 1964, he jumped out of a second-floor window during a fire at 4136 Gladys St. where the family lived. All his brothers and sisters at the time—James Jr., 11, Denise, 9; Kevin, 8; Patricia, 6; Tyrone, 4; Steve, 5; and Christina, 1—died in the flames. His parents were burned.

Friday, Gloria Alford, 50, sat in their neat brick bungalow on South

Keith Alford

Princeton Avenue trying to understand why 8 of her 10 children had been taken from her.

"I'd much rather it had been me than Keith," she sobbed. "He had so much to live for."

"I can't help but ask myself, 'Why me all the time?' I try to keep the faith. I believe in God. Why me all the time? I just can't figure it out."

Her two remaining sons — Daryl, 13, and Derrick, 12 — were born since the fire.

ALFORD BELIEVES Keith died from what the Marine Corps called "nocturnal seizures." [Alfred calls them some sort of epilepsy.] He thinks Keith developed the disorder while assigned to helicopter rescue teams in Viet Nam. It led to a medical discharge.

"These type of seizure comes only at night," Mrs. Alford said. "We only saw it happen once; he shook all over and then just passed."

Alford said he believes his son died shortly after dinner Thursday night.

"I had asked him if he was going out, and he said, 'No, Mom, that was a really good meal. I'm full,'" Mrs. Alford said.

Keith will be buried Monday next to his seven brothers and sisters in Lincoln Cemetery, 123d Street and Kedzie Avenue.

"I've only had the will to go to the gravesites twice since it [the fire] happened," Alford said. "Now I have to go again."

Keith Passes

Left To Right Darryl, Derrick, James,
Gloria and James's Mother Martha-Lovejoy

James Loved His Job

Darryl L. Alford

Derrick D. Alford

James Celebrating As Always

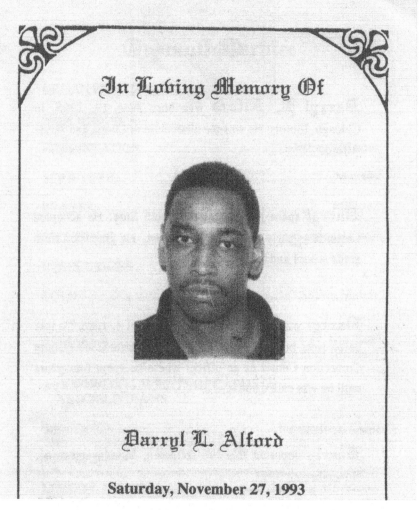

Darryl L. Alford Obituary

In Loving Memory
of

Sgt. James E. Alford

August 12, 1926   February 9, 2000

Sgt. James Alford Obituary

OUR BELOVED GRANDFATHER

To us you were our daddy. When God called our own fathers home, without a shadow or doubt, you stepped up to the plate instantly. You vowed to be the best dad you could be to us. You never let us down. Even in your last days, you told us to continue on with the strength and the courage you have instilled in us. For you will always be the "Wind Beneath Our Wings." We know you are watching us from above. Tell our fathers, Keith and Darryl, hello for us. Your fight is over. We love you, but God loves you most!

Our Sweet Daddy, May You Rest In Peace!

Felicia, Darryl, Keith, and Denise

Celebrating the Life of

Sunrise
April 7, 1928

Sunset
January 18, 2007

Gloria E. Alford

Gloria E. Alford Obituary

James & Gloria
The Alford Family Lives on...

REFERENCES

Birmingham Post-Herald; article, February, 22nd, 1964 Edition.

Chicago Sun-Times, article, February 22nd, 1964 Edition.

ChicagoHistory.org – Police, 1900-1960.

Chicago Tribune, article, February 22nd, 1964 Edition.

Chicago Tribune, article *by Robert Enstad*, 1978 Edition.

Mass rally, sponsored by the Civic Liberty League of Il, April 2nd, 1964.

Timeline of African American history, Wikipedia, 1920–2018.

Yeaton Reporting Company, March, 1966.

ABOUT THE AUTHOR

FELICIA ALFORD is a first-time author and the mother of two beautiful children. She is also a proud native of the South Side of Chicago. Felicia has cultivated a successful career, spanning over twenty years of elevated leadership and brand management, with an accomplished tenure as a corporate sales executive in the beauty industry. She is known by her colleagues as someone who is dedicated and takes on each task with tenacity and a strong commitment. Felicia applied that same determination in fulfilling her goal of writing a personal true story that she hopes the readers find compelling and enjoy!

Made in the USA
Monee, IL
24 March 2020